THE HERALD
DIARY

WITH

THE HERALD DIARY

Panda To Your Every Desire

Ken Smith

BLACK & WHITE PUBLISHING

First published 2011
by Black & White Publishing Ltd
29 Ocean Drive, Edinburgh EH6 6JL

1 3 5 7 9 10 8 6 4 2   11 12 13 14

ISBN: 978 1 84502 358 4

A CIP catalogue record for this book is available from the British Library.

Typeset by Ellipsis Digital Limited, Glasgow
Printed and bound by MPG Books Ltd, Bodmin

Contents

Introduction

Who could blame any Scot who parodied Rikki Fulton's character, the Rev. I.M. Jolly, and went around declaiming, "Ah've had a helluva year"?

If they weren't worried about the economy, petrol prices shooting up or the disappearance of sunny summer weather, they couldn't even rely on the football to cheer them up.

So instead Scots did what they always do in times of trouble – they cracked jokes about it.

Even better, they then sent the jokes, funny stories and daft encounters to *The Herald* newspaper's Diary column for everyone to share.

We are indebted to the readers for doing so, and in return here are the very best of the funny tales told, and amusing pictures snapped, for your enjoyment.

We suspect that even the Rev. I.M. Jolly might have smiled a little if he had been given this book.

1.
To See Ourselves

You don't always need haggis and whisky in front of you in order to quote Rabbie Burns. When Scots go abroad, or visitors come to Scotland, it reminds us: "O would some power the giftie gie us, to see ourselves as others see us."

SCOTTISH hospitality and friendliness is famous all over the world, we know that, and Willie Aitken from Ottawa proves it.

Willie was visiting friends in Stornoway and went into the chip shop after the bar closed and ordered a hamburger supper.

The lady wrapped it up, then said conspiratorially: "The hamburgers aren't very good tonight, so I've given you two."

HURRICANE IRENE was one of the largest storms in years to hit the eastern seaboard of America. Reader Alastair Breckenridge contacted friends in Philadelphia to check they were okay.

His friends replied that the city had suffered its wettest August since records began.

It had been so bad, he added, there were plans to change the city's name to Scotland.

A READER in Sydney swears that a young toper in his local bar announced: "I got attacked by a great white shark out on the surf."

"Did you punch it on the nose," asked an interested onlooker.

"No," replied the swimmer, "he just attacked me for no reason."

MIKE RITCHIE, watching the severe weather conditions on America's Eastern seaboard, tells us: "Hurricane Irene has been downgraded to a Scottish summer."

A READER in the United States was listening to the presenter on a TV show who announced: "Coming up after the break – how to save money on vacations. Don't go away."

"Good advice," thought our reader.

SOMETIMES we like a joke because it's just plain daft. So thank you John Daly in Houston for telling us about the two American tourists ordering horse steaks in a Glasgow restaurant.

"We don't eat horse over here," the waitress told them.

"So how come that guy over there just ordered mare soup?" asked one of the Yanks.

NEW YORK taxi drivers have a tough reputation. David Speedie in the city recounts: "My wife, on her first visit by car to Manhattan, got hopelessly lost. She pulled up at traffic lights, next to a taxi driver, and asked directions. Without looking at her he replied, 'If you don't know New York, lady, take a cab.'"

A LONDON correspondent tells us he was in his local boozer when the TV news carried the headline: "Winds of 100mph batter Scotland."

At that a local loudmouth opined: "That won't bother the Jocks. They love everything as long as it's battered."

BRUCE MACGREGOR of Scottish music group Blazin' Fiddles was having a few libations after a gig in Perth with members of a Polish band on the bill when the Polish drummer leaned forward and said: "I like your wooden legs."

Bruce laughed nervously, tapped his legs and said: "I think you mean hollow legs," but the Pole insisted, "No, I like your wooden legs."

Says Bruce: "I was a bit perplexed. Blokes don't normally talk about my legs.

"I asked again, and he slowed down and waved his arms about. 'I like this country – I like the woods and lakes.'"

THE EARTHQUAKE in the eastern US has naturally excited a lot of nervy Americans. As one of them tweeted afterwards: "Gosh! It's only been like a half hour – and already I've finished my 15-day supply of emergency food."

A BEARSDEN reader tells us an American girl was staying with his family over Christmas, who was taken aback by the pessimism of some Scots. When she was waiting for a train into Glasgow, a fellow traveller asked: "How are you?" and she replied: "Can't complain."

The chap then asked: "Why not?"

AS BARACK OBAMA'S presidency loses its glister, John McBride in Texas sees a car sticker with a picture of a smiling and waving George W. Bush with the caption: "Missing me yet?"

FRANK PIGNATELLI, retired to France, tells us crime drama *Taggart* is very popular on local TV, and is shown with French sub-titles. The problem is that the Glaswegian dialogue can sometimes be a challenge for the translators.

Two characters were coming out of a chip shop, says Frank. One of them opened his bag of chips and barked: "Where's ma pickled onion?" The French translation on screen said simply: "Bon appétit!"

NEWS of the bad weather in Scotland reached America as a reader sends us a cutting from his local newspaper that included the letter: "I've just heard from a friend in Scotland. He says it has been snowing heavily for three days now. His wife has done nothing but stare through the window.

"If it doesn't stop soon he'll probably have to let her in."

GARY JOHNSTON in Australia was talking to a fellow ex-pat, Billy, about how you can tell if you have been fully absorbed into Australian life. Billy went to a bookshelf and returned with a tome entitled *Blokes and Their Sheds*. "If you think this is about garden outhouses, you're definitely an Aussie," Billy told him.

"If, on the other hand, you assume it's a book about hairstyles, you're still essentially Scottish."

AN AMERICAN visitor to the UK says when he was visiting Stratford-upon-Avon he asked a local what St George's Day was all about.

"It's like St Patrick's Day," the chap replied. "But without all the fuss."

NEWS from abroad, and we note that Frank Buckles, the last surviving American soldier from World War One, has died at the age of 110. We mention it as we've always liked the answer Frank once gave when he was asked the secret of a long life. "When you think you're dying," Frank replied, "don't."

A LESMAHAGOW reader visiting friends in Texas felt a sticker she saw on a woman's car over there could equally apply to harassed mothers over here. It read: "If a woman's place is in the home, why am I always in this car?"

POLISH workers – they've been great for Scotland, although there have been misunderstandings. A reader who works in a major Scottish hotel tells us about the Polish receptionist who was on duty when an elderly American guest called reception as her husband wasn't feeling well, and she asked for a doctor.

"American or European?" asked the receptionist. She asked for American.

Five minutes later, the Polish chap arrived at the door with an American adaptor.

A READER in Maryland, USA, tells us her dentist has a sign on the receptionist's counter which says: "Please be nice to our dentists. They have fillings, too."

IT'S GREAT when readers in America send us cuttings of so-called Scottish jokes from their newspapers. The latest reads: "An American businessman in Glasgow walked into a restaurant and asked the waitress what the special was. 'Roast and rice,' the Scottish miss replied in a heavy brogue.

"'You certainly do roll your Rs,' the businessman observed.

"'I suppose,' she giggled, 'but only when I wear high heels.'"

All we could think was: roast and rice? Who would ever serve that?

BBC SCOTLAND'S health correspondent Eleanor Bradford took some Ozzy friends to Oban. She warned them that the beefburgers on sale in a local chippy were not like the beefburgers they were used to in Australia. Her fears were confirmed when the Australians asked the woman in the chip shop if the beefburgers were fresh.

"Aye," she replied. "Straight out the freezer, and we freshly fry them."

CAM HAMILTON, whose late father had a grocer's shop in Lanark near the River Clyde, tells us his dad, on more than one occasion, had American visitors, fans of the late Harry Lauder it seems, who came in to the shop to ask: "Where can we find Gloamin?"

A PERTHSHIRE reader back from a holiday in America saw an auld fella at a shopping mall get into a car which had a sticker on the back window stating: "I'm retired. I was tired yesterday. I'm tired again today."

AUSTRALIA was having a tough time of it with fires and floods, and one of the most heartbreaking stories from the floods was the *Morning Bulletin* newspaper in Queensland reporting that "30,000 pigs were floating down the Dawson River".

The newspaper put an apology in the following day which read: "What piggery owner Sid Everingham said was thirty sows and pigs."

TALKING of Australia, Bill Arnott tells us that the Queensland flooding and cyclone damage means banana prices rocketing locally due to the damage to crops. He tells us that after the last cyclone in the area, a shop in the town of Nambour put a notice in its window stating, "No bananas kept on these premises overnight."

A READER now living in South Carolina couldn't wait to tell us that his daughter's new English teacher is named Paige Turner.

WE HAVE long been admirers of Australian plain speaking. A report in *The Herald* about allowing tattooing in Scottish prisons referred to previous Australian research. A member of the Scottish Prison Service tells us: "Our study is called 'Tattooing in Scottish Prisons: A health care needs assessment'.

"The Australian university research published in the *Australian Health Review* was entitled 'Jaggers in the Pokey'."

WE HAVE made fun of Americans visiting Scotland, and now a reader living in the United States returns the compliment by sending us a cutting from a Texan newspaper which states: "A dying Scotsman on his death bed looked up and asked if his wife was there. 'Yes, dear, I'm right next to you,' she replied. 'Are my children here?' he asked. 'Yes, daddy, we're all here,' they said.

"'Then why the heck is the light on in the kitchen?' he asked."

A GLASGOW student spent the summer working at a wildlife park in Canada. He had to tell owners of soft-topped cars that they couldn't drive through the park in case the bears tore at the roof.

"How about if I just put the top down?" one woman asked him.

NOT THAT we are making any inferences about Americans and their IQs, but reader Stephen Gold was in the Museum of Modern Art in New York where one of the exhibition spaces had a sign stating:

"Sponsored by Banana Republic".

A woman who had been reading it with a quizzical expression turned and asked her husband: "Harry, do you think this is the fashion store or the country?"

A UNITED STATES member on a Land Rover owners' discussion group told the old gag of the Grand Canyon being started by a Scot digging for a dropped penny. By the end of the discussion, the Americans had decided that all Scottish inventions were inspired by a desire to save money:

Alexander Graham Bell invented the telephone to save on bus fares visiting people. John Logie Baird invented the TV to save buying cinema tickets. Sir Robert Watson-Watt developed radar so that the authorities could make money fining speeding motorists. Alexander Bain invented the fax machine to save on postage.

And our favourite: Sir James Dewar invented the vacuum flask to save buying his coffee from Starbucks.

2.
The Little Darlings

Scots love their children – no matter what they might tell their friends about them. As one cynical mother put it: "I wanted to have children while my parents were still young enough to look after them."

Here are some of the little darlings' stories.

PROOF that our children grow up too quickly comes from reader Stephen Macleod who was chatting to a Kilmarnock minister who visited a local primary school during the bad weather. With snow still on the ground, one of the primary seven sidled up to the minister and asked: "Do you think the snow will affect the going at Cheltenham?"

A READER visiting a council swimming pool watched as the chap in front paid for himself and his older child, but said the younger one was only three, which meant she could get in for free.

As the girl seemed quite tall for this age, the chap behind the counter asked when she would be four, the age at which a ticket had to be bought.

"When the recession's over," her dad replied.

TALES of upbraiding children remind Gordon Walker of being in a newsagents under the Hielanman's Umbrella in Argyle Street when a wee Glesga wummin with a toddler and a five-year-old boy was fishing in her purse for change.

Her son, staring at a lad's mag, asked: "How come that lady's boobs are bigger than yours?"

Gordon tells us: "The mother, without missing a beat, responded, 'Because you ate mine, son.'"

JOHN SWORD at Glasgow's meat market tells us of a friend's young son keenly watching a neighbour who had called in for a cup of tea. His staring made her feel uncomfortable until she finally asked the lad what he was looking at.

He then explained: "My parents say you drink like a fish."

A BEARSDEN reader tells us their twenty-something son has moved back in with them as he says it will give him the opportunity to save up for the deposit on a flat.

She now thinks he will be there for a while after tidying up his bedroom and coming across a large glass jar full of coins with the label "flat deposit" taped to it.

A JORDANHILL reader says he and his wife were delighted with a new baby-sitter who told them when they returned from a night out that she had got all three of their children to go to bed by 9pm.

They told her that was very impressive as they could never manage that themselves on a non-school night, and asked what her secret was.

"Simple," she told them. "I put the clock on your mantelpiece forward by two hours."

A CLYDEBANK reader took his eight-year-old son for his first game of golf. When the two of them got held up by a four-ball in front, his son asked what a four-ball was. His father explained it was four players playing together, which can slow things down.

As they waited, two chaps playing the hole behind them caught up, and asked what the hold-up was. "There are four men over there," explained his young son, "having four-play."

Says our reader: "Have to wait a few years to explain why he caused such hilarity."

MAW ONE and Maw Two, overheard on a Glasgow bus.

One says her son is getting too much of "that healthy fruit" at school. Maw Two asks, why are you complaining?

Because, comes the answer, when her boy gets home from school for dinner, he's so full of fruit that he "cannae finish his chips".

YOU NEVER know what you are going to hear when you ask the audience at an Edinburgh Fringe show a question.

Compere Billy Kirkwood at the kids' comedy show *Toybox* at The Stand, asked one youngster where he was from and what it was like. The boy, who was about eight, replied: "I'm from Aberdour." He then added, with a shake of his young head: "Frankly, the village isn't what it used to be."

A READER at Clydebank's shopping centre witnessed the latest debate on healthy eating. A young girl asked her mum: "Why do vegetables taste horrible?" Her harassed mother told her: "Sometimes things that taste horrible are good for you."

"Like Auntie Anne-Marie's cooking?" was the devastating riposte from the young girl.

"I DIDN'T want my son to become a juggler," said the chap in the pub the other night. "It's frightening how many of them end up on the street."

MIKE RITCHIE tells us of a female friend, a long-suffering mum to three kids between the ages of nine and fifteen.

She's given up trying to communicate with them. She stands at the foot of the stairs and shrieks at them until she becomes hoarse, yet still they ignore her.

The solution? "The easiest way is just to ring their mobiles – they answer those quickly enough."

AN EDINBURGH mother tells us: "Now I know why it was worthwhile teaching my little son what slots the round, square and triangle blocks of wood went in his Early Learning Centre toy.

"Ten years later, when I couldn't set up my computer along with the printer and broadband, he was able to take all the oddly shaped ends of wires and work out where they fitted."

A READER in a Glasgow fast-food restaurant was disturbed by a little lad yelling at his mother: "You don't know what I want! You don't know what I want!"

The boy's mother looked down and calmly replied: "Darren, you're only four. You don't even know what you want."

A READER felt sorry for the mother taking her young children into Glasgow by bus during the school holidays who passed the time by starting a rhyming game.

"I'll go first," she said. "Cat."

"Mat," replied one child.

"Your turn," said the mum.

"Gorilla," said the other child, and our reader watched as the mother's face frowned in speechlessness.

READER Robert Gardner tells us that his grandson had swallowed a five pence piece, and the medical advice was that it could take up to three days for it to reappear. However, the boy's mum texted Robert to say it was retrieved just the next day.

"Just like his dad," Robert texted back. "He couldn't hold on to money for long either."

NOT EVERY young worker is aware of the needs of mothers, it seems. A reader was in a Glasgow city-centre coffee shop when the woman in front of him in the queue carrying a baby in her arms, asked if they had a high chair.

The young chap serving her furrowed his brow before finally replying: "I think the ones by the front window are pretty high."

LYNDA NICOLSON tells us: "The other night my four-year-old niece asked, 'For a treat, do you have anything for me to eat that isn't good for me?'"

A TEACHER says one of her young charges excitedly told her that her mum had given birth to twins. Chatting about them, the teacher asked who they looked like. "Each other," said the confused youngster.

RULE 2

ALL CHILDREN MUST WEAR SAFETY BELTS AROUND THEIR WASTE

CHILDREN are getting more precocious, it seems. Kate Woods tells us about a friend's granddaughter who was asked by granny what her first day at nursery was like.

"Good," the little one replied. "I'm the prettiest girl in the class."

"Who said that?" asked granny.

"No-one," she said. "I just looked at all the others."

SOME newspaper headlines from the world of sport remind Frank de Pellett of the line about the wee boy telling his aunt: "When I grow up, I want tae be a fitba' player."

"Don't be daft," she replied. "Ye cannae dae both."

SCOTLAND'S heavy snow brought out some neighbourly camaraderie, with folk checking on the elderly nearby. It reminded one reader of the classic – i.e. old – story of the housewife wanting to check on the pensioner next door.

She sent her eight-year-old son "to see how old Mrs McLeod is". He returned to say that Mrs McLeod said her age was none of her business.

"WE WERE having a family argument when my daughter said she had nothing in common with the rest of us, and asked if she was adopted," said the chap in the pub.

"So I told her she was – but that it didn't work out and the other family brought her back."

A STORY about Radio 4 reminds a fan of the station in Bearsden of taking his teenage daughter out for a driving lesson in his car. Thinking that she should adjust the mirror before driving off, he asked her: "What's the first thing you should do?"

"Change the radio station," she replied.

JEFF MILLER at Hampden Cars picked up a dental nurse who told him about her boss being perplexed by a young child who faithfully brushed her teeth twice a day, but was still having a lot of decay.

Further investigation by the dentist uncovered the fact that the child didn't like the taste of minty toothpaste, so her mother allowed her to use sugary cola afterwards as a mouthwash.

ZUMBA, the latest fitness craze using energetic South American dancing, is not known by everyone.

An Ayrshire mother tells us about her daughter telling her papa that she had to leave early to go to Zumba with her pal. The auld fella told her it was one of Michael Caine's best films – but wasn't it a bit gory for two young girls?

JIM NICOL in Lenzie tells us of a friend's seven-year-old son wanting to help his dad with the *Evening Times* crossword. The dad had mixed emotions when the lad looked at the clue "Raining heavily" which began with P, ending in "ing" and suggested "pissing", rather than the expected answer "pouring", as at least it fitted. But where did he learn such language?

A YOUNG mum was overheard telling her friends on the Glasgow to Edinburgh train: "I caught my husband staring at our son in his cot with an obvious look of pride and affection on his face.

"He then spoiled it all by saying, 'I can't believe we got such a good cot for under a hundred quid.'"

A READER at a play park heard a father shout at his young son, who was keeping the toys to himself: "Sonny! Share! Sonny! Share!" Inevitably, one of the other parents started singing: "I got you babe."

3.
From Shipyards To Call Centres

Employment in Scotland has gone from shipyards to call centres. But thankfully the humour still remains.

GOVERNMENT plans to cut the number of people claiming incapacity benefit have not gone unnoticed by the staff at Maryhill's Jobcentre Plus in Glasgow who will have to implement the policy.

They now refer to their office as Lourdes.

"I GOT woken up today by some idiot banging on my window," said the chap in the pub the other night. "I was raging. There were two other tellers who could have cashed his pension."

A PSYCHIATRIST tells us that when she is buttonholed at a party and asked what she does to help people with low self-esteem, her quick answer is: "I tell them they should become politicians. That usually solves it."

FIND OUT WHAT'S HAPPENING IN MOTHERWELL

tv/motherwell   MASS UNEMPLOYMENT.   stv ▸ MOTHERWELL ◂ BE PART OF IT.

A HUMAN resources worker in Glasgow's call-centre sector tells us he interviewed a chap who had been fired from his last two jobs. When he queried this with him, the bold chap replied: "Well at least it shows I'm not a quitter."

COLIN MACFARLANE'S book *Gorbals Diehards*, about growing up there in the sixties, tells of shipyard worker Jimmy who explained a fellow worker was nicknamed Brewer's Droop as his name was Wullie Falls. More opaque was the foreman every worker called Such. That came about, explained Jimmy, when he was promoted to foreman and told the men: "I'm now the boss, and from now on I want to be addressed as such."

TALKING of shipyards, reader Jim Morrison reminds us of the classic gag: "A Clydebank chap invited a young lady to his flat for a nightcap. 'See that carpet? It's aff the *QE2*. And see that chest of drawers? That's aff the *Queen Mary*. And see that sideboard? It's aff the *Queen Elizabeth*,' he said.

"'Is that right?' said the young lady. 'Is this some kind of boat hoose?'

"'Naw,' replied the chap, 'I just rent it aff the cooncil.'"

OUR STORY about shipyard workers with sticky fingers reminds Mark Johnston of a neighbour who kept a *Queen Mary* coffeepot from the final voyage of the Clyde steamer before it became a floating restaurant in London. Says Mark: "Unfortunately, during a break-in a few years later, the coffeepot was stolen.

"As my neighbour was giving a list of the stolen objects to the policeman, he hesitated when asked how much he paid for the coffeepot.

"Picking up on this, the policeman simply told him, 'Shall we just say it fell off the back of a boat, Sir?'"

AS FINAL year students start applying for jobs, we pass on a tip from recruitment company Career Builders which says that many CVs are automatically rejected by companies because of folk having unprofessional e-mail addresses.

"One candidate," says the company, "had an e-mail address with 'lovesbeer' in it. Another candidate had put God down as a referee, but alas did not provide a contact phone number."

A READER tells us he overheard two women discussing the new staffer in their office. "She looks a bit like Paris Hilton," said one. "More Paris Travelodge," replied her colleague.

CAMPAIGNING at Govan Cross to save the aircraft carrier contracts, Glasgow City Council leader Gordon Matheson was beckoned over by an elderly Govanite. The old boy said that in the 1970s his wife had anxiously asked union leader Jimmy Reid if any shipyard workers were to be laid off as she was worried about her man's job.

Jimmy told her: "We're fighting for every man, Mary, but it looks like six fitters are being made redundant."

"That's all right," said Mary. "My husband's only five foot six."

OUR STORY of Jimmy Reid and working class rights remind Ian Wilson of dismantling a crane at Blairs defunct steelworks in Govan. After the final staff had been paid off, Ian noticed chalked on the wall in large letters: "Those who work and do their best, get their books alang wi' the rest".

WE WON'T name the Lothian company where a reader tells us one of the staff, after going on a health kick, had lost a sizeable amount of weight. One of the engineers complimented her and she replied: "Thanks. So you noticed?"

He perhaps should have left it at that, instead of adding: "Well, your arse used to have its own post code."

AUTUMN, apart from being when the leaves fall, is the busiest time for after-dinner speakers.

Tom Munro tells us former police officer John McKelvie was speaking after the former footballer and rascal Frank McAvennie at the Inverclyde Amateurs anniversary dinner.

John commented it wasn't the first time he had followed McAvennie – but it was the first time that Frank had been aware of it.

GLASGOW entrepreneur Charan Gill's Hottest Night of the Year charity dinner at the Hilton involved business people trying stand-up comedy.

The winner was fashion agency owner Jack Konopate, who was praised by judge Tam Cowan for being controversial.

Declared Jack: "I have family back in Israel who own a pharmaceutical business which makes Israel's best-known cure for indigestion.

"Maybe you've heard of it – it's called Jewish Settlers."

RUNNER-UP Gaynor Turner of jewellers Macintyres of Edinburgh told the audience that the Scottish team at the Commonwealth Games had eighteen gold medals, eleven silver and twenty-two bronze, adding: "That'll serve the Canadians right for leaving their lockers open."

FORMER Rangers and Scotland keeper Andy Goram was at a supporters' dinner in Dundee, having accepted the invitation by telling the organiser, "Look after me if you can . . . and remember, I like a nice red wine."

So Andy's at the table and is delighted to spot six tempting bottles of a really nice Rioja.

"The guy's done me proud," he thinks and, before you know it, Andy and his companions have opened and finished one bottle. Then two. Then three. Four. Five.

Then the night's big attraction, the raffle, starts. The third item? Six bottles of a really nice Rioja. Which by this time is – well, irretrievable.

Which is why a slightly shamefaced Mr Goram made speedy amends to the organiser by getting tickets for an Old Firm game.

WHO SAYS funeral directors don't have a sense of humour? A guest at a dinner attended by the Provost of Renfrewshire and other dignitaries to mark the centenary of Renfrew funeral directors Walter Johnston & Sons, tells us one speaker recounted the classic yarn of the young boy being off school, and being asked by his teacher where he had been. He replied that his dad had been in an accident and got burned.

"I'm sorry," replied his teacher. "I hope it was nothing serious."

"Well, miss," he replied, "they don't mess about at the crematorium."

CELEBRATING Dunfermline's promotion to the Scottish Premier League is the club's legendary director of football Jim Leishman. He told a fundraising dinner in Glasgow for Epilepsy Scotland that as a young player he could have signed for Liverpool, Manchester United or Chelsea.

"But none of them wanted me," he added, "so I signed for Dunfermline."

INCIDENTALLY, one of the hotly contested auction items at the Epilepsy Scotland dinner was a day's fishing at Balmoral, including the services of a ghillie.

Denis MacCann, boss of the new Hotel Indigo in Glasgow, helpfully explained to the Diary: "Did you know that 'ghillie' is Gaelic for sitting on the riverbank laughing while you watch someone with a fishing rod make a complete idiot of themselves?"

A HELENSBURGH reader was at a business dinner recently where the guest speaker was from a leading building firm.

"Rome wasn't built in a day," he told his audience, before adding: "Although that was the builder's original estimate."

Enjoy our champagne
reception this weekend

All visitors this weekend
will be entered into a
prize drawer to win
£1000 towards a dream
bedroom or kitchen.

A READER couldn't help smiling when he was at a business reception in Edinburgh, and watched a chap go up to an American woman with the name "Twila" on her badge and say: "That's a name you don't hear every day."

"Actually, I do," she coolly replied.

GLASGOW'S entrepreneurs are alive and well, says reader James Davitt, who was stopped on his return to the big open car park behind St Enoch's by a chap who asked if he had any time left on his pay and display ticket.

Says James: "Thinking I was doing my good deed for the day, I obliged.

"As I was driving away, I noticed he was at one of the ticket machines, selling my ticket at a no doubt discounted rate, to another punter.

"Some Glaswegians could teach those Apprentice candidates a thing or two."

A SCOTTISH website provider tells us that on their registration page they have a box for the email address of potential customers, followed by a second box marked "confirm email".

One subscriber had simply typed in the second box: "Yes, above email address is correct."

READER Jim McGrouther hears on Sky news that Japanese electronics company Sony is throwing itself into the tablet market.

He wonders how worried Scottish confectioners should be.

THERE'S not been much humour in the Glasgow housing market of late, but an estate agent did tell us that he was showing a couple a flat in the West End recently where all the rooms were off an imposing 40ft hall.

When the wife asked her husband if they should put in an offer for it, hubby told her: "I'm certainly in it for the long hall."

IT'S NOT often we are given a gag by an economist, so we must pass it on. "An Irishman, a German, a Portuguese and a Greek walk into a bar," he said.

"And the German ended up paying."

WHEN spring is in the air, suburban dwellers turn their minds to extensions and conservatories. We remember the chap in Bearsden who was building an extension when he was approached by a chap offering to sell him suspiciously cheap bricks.

Not wishing to overlook a bargain, he agreed – only to discover the brick seller had taken the bricks already stacked in the back of his garden and delivered them to the front.

When he went to the police, they warned him that if they were to arrest the thief, they would have to arrest him as well for buying stolen goods.

WE ASKED a Glasgow businessman who regularly checks his Twitter account what the fascination was, and he told us: "It's a bit like when you are bored at home and you open the fridge to see if there is anything interesting. There isn't, but it still doesn't stop you checking again twenty minutes later."

4.
Affairs Of The Heart

The average Scot dislikes talking about his emotions and would rather make a joke about relationships. That might not be good for his relationships, but it works out fine for The Diary.

"I ASKED my girlfriend what she wanted for her birthday," said the chap in the pub the other night. "So with a big smile she held up her left hand and wiggled her third finger."

He then added: "Gloves it is then."

IT'S A difficult time for relationships with couples thrown together for days over Christmas and New Year. One chap confessed to us that his wife angrily turned to him the other day and declared: "Why have you ignored the fact that I've not been speaking to you for three days?"

The surprised chap could only reply: "I thought we were just getting along."

THE JOKER in the pub the other night claimed: "The wife asked what I was doing on the computer and I said I was looking for cheap flights."

He added: "She got all excited, which is strange, as she's never shown any interest in darts before."

AN AYRSHIRE reader tells us about the chap turning up at his golf club after being off on holiday. "Did you have a good time?" he was asked.

"The first day of my break," he told them, "the wife winked at me and said she couldn't wait to get me in the bedroom."

He then added: "When I got there I found six litres of paint and a roller."

RETURNING home in the evening rush hour to Helensburgh, a reader heard a chap on the train tell a pal: "The wife tells me I snore when I'm sleeping. But that's rubbish. No one at work has ever mentioned it."

A SOUTH-SIDE lady out for a night with her chums showed them the text her husband had sent the night before when he had been out with his pals.

The brave, but foolhardy chap had texted: "Just having a final pint. Will be home in half an hour. If not back by then simply read this text again."

THE DATING game, it seems, is still a jungle. Our attention is drawn to the website crapdate.com where people can record their worst

experiences. We were taken with the woman who succinctly wrote: "Worst date has to be the guy who pretended to be a doctor. When rumbled, he pretended he was a secret agent posing as a doctor."

SOMEONE not winning any gallantry awards was the best man at a wedding who telephoned the office that produced a road safety poster plastered on the rear of Edinburgh buses.

The caller explained that the poster featured a street scene containing the bride's house. He asked if he could get a copy of the poster, then added: "I want to say in my speech that every time I see the bride she always reminds me of the back of a bus."

A CHAP in the pub the other night declared: "The wife says we would have less arguments if I wasn't so pedantic."

He added: "So I told her that surely she meant 'fewer'."

"THE GIRLFRIEND," said the chap in the pub, "was constantly nagging me about getting married, so to shut her up I said we could have a summer wedding."

"July?" asked his mate.

"Of course I did," the chap replied.

WE DON'T know how his relationship is faring, but a chap was overheard by a reader in a Glasgow pub declaring on the first of April: "April Fool's Day is great."

He then added: "My girlfriend totally believes I'm on my way to collect her at the airport."

ON MOTHER'S DAY a chap in Holytown, Lanarkshire, was heard telling his mates: "I gave the wife a real treat for Mother's Day – I allowed her to use the TV remote for ten minutes."

TRYING to think of something interesting to tell his mates, the chap in the pub announced: "My new girlfriend once went out with a professional clown."

"I guess you've got some pretty big shoes to fill," a pal replied.

WE MENTIONED that misogyny was still rife in Scotland. A reader tells us of being in a Motherwell bar the other week when a chap announced: "I complimented my wife on having an hour-glass figure."

He then added: "I didn't tell her it was because all the weight is slowly moving to the bottom."

THE BAD weather brings out the caring side in us. Alistair Magill passed an elderly couple tottering into East Kilbride shopping centre. "I was impressed," he said, "to see the husband taking his wife's arm in his, as the ground was slippery with the new snow.

"Only when I got closer did I hear him say nice and clearly, 'Now if you fall, let go of me, as you're no taking me wi' ye.'

"Chivalry and wedded bliss."

"I'M WORRIED that the wife is losing her mind," said the chap in the golf club bar the other night.

"She keeps on telling me that she's talking to a brick wall."

"THE WIFE and I were talking about making wills," said the chap in the pub. "I told her I would leave everything to her."

He added: "She told me, 'You already do, you lazy so-and-so.'"

MEN: not always the cleverest of people. A reader heard a young chap in a Glasgow pub being told by a female friend that she didn't think his pal liked her. Seemingly, popularity matters to some women. Anyway, what our reader enjoyed was the chap's reply: "That's not true. In fact, he was actually defending you the other day when I was slagging you off."

MOST folk went back to work in early January after what can be a stressful time at home. Bruce Skivington tells us about having a house full of visitors when the lady of the house ranted about someone using the good towel, which she was trying to keep nice for guests in the bathroom.

When Bruce asked the family what was wrong, he was told that mother had "irritable towel syndrome".

A HYNDLAND reader tells us his wife announced that, to try to give herself an incentive to lose weight, she would treat herself to a new pair of shoes for every 10lbs she lost.

He now realises that replying: "That's a lot of new shoes," wasn't the encouragement she was looking for.

A HELENSBURGH reader, out for a walk with his wife, drew her attention to a couple holding hands on the promenade and remarked: "They look like a happily married couple."

He was surprised when she replied: "You can't be so certain. After all, they might be saying the same about us."

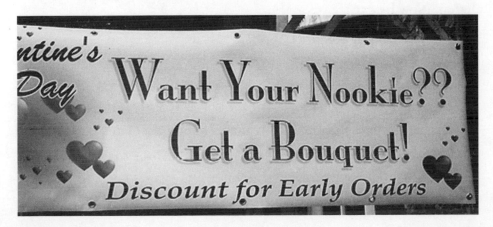

A READER overhears a group of women in the West End discussing their sex lives. "Does your husband ever send you saucy texts?" asked one.

After thinking, one replied: "He did once text to remind me to get Heinz ketchup on the way home."

A RENFREWSHIRE reader discovered how complicated courting has become these days when he heard two girls at a multi-screen cinema excitedly discussing the young chap taking the tickets.

"He's so cute," declared one. "Ask him furris phone number," suggested her friend.

"Naw. Ahm too shy," her pal replied.

"Well how about asking another worker what his name is as you want to report him to the manager for something, then just stalk him on Facebook," her friend further suggested.

A BAILLIESTON reader visiting her parents mentioned to her mother that her dad seemed to be losing his hearing.

"Things haven't really changed," her mum replied. "Before, he didn't listen. Now he can't."

THE BOLD lad in the pub the other night stated: "Just reserved a table for my wife for Valentine's Day."

He then added: "I normally buy flowers and chocolates, but Ikea had a sale on."

THAT inevitably reminds us of the morose chap in the pub who told his mates that he had mixed up his Valentine cards. As he told them: "Now my girlfriend thinks I love her, and my wife thinks I want to sleep with her."

VALENTINE'S DAY, and, no, we don't believe the loudmouth in the pub last night who declared: "I got the wife a Valentine's present that really took her breath away.

"She's been needing a treadmill for years."

THAT reminds us of the woman who noticed her husband standing on the bathroom scales and sucking his ample stomach in.

"That's not going to help," she said.

"It does if you want to read the numbers," he replied.

A CHAP whose wife was in hospital bumped into a pal who asked him how his wife was.

"Critical," he replied.

His shocked pal told him: "But I thought she was in for a simple procedure?"

"She is," said the chap. "But she's already complained about the food being cold, the sheets being threadbare, the toilet being dirty, and the staff being unhelpful."

A RETIRED reader changing at Green's gym at Giffnock was chatting to a pal when he noticed his friend had a number of bruises on his shin. "You're not still playing football at your age are you?" he asked.

When his friend said no, our reader pointed at the bruises, and the chap told him: "I play a lot of bridge with the wife as my partner."

"DID YOU hear that Duncan's gettin' married?" asked the loudmouth in a Glasgow pub at the weekend.

"Ah telt him how happy ma marriage had made me," he continued.

"But he's still goin' through wi' it anyway."

A YOUNG lad going to work on the bus in Glasgow was heard telling his pal about the wedding he had been a guest at. "Ah don't think it's goin' tae last," he opined.

When asked why, he explained: "The bride wiz textin' a' through the groom's speech."

"MY WIFE'S always nagging me for not taking the bins out," said the loudmouth in the pub. "So I gave in. Mind you I got some very strange looks when I arrived at the cinema."

"THE WIFE treats me like a god," said the loudmouth in the pub the other night. "She takes very little notice of my existence until she wants something."

A READER realised how rocky the path of true love is in Glasgow when he heard a young girl on Byres Road snap at her boyfriend: "You're always slagging me off."

"No I'm not," he replied. "When did I do that?"

"In the pub," she told him.

"You're supposed to slag folk off in the pub," he told her exasperatedly.

5.
Why Glasgow Loves Zombies

We may no longer have the legendary Five Past Eight shows in Glasgow with English comedians being chased off stage, but Scots still love a bit of celebrity. When Brad Pitt wanted to make a zombie film in Glasgow no one objected, with many Glaswegians themselves bragging it was filmed in Glasgow as there were many local extras who wouldn't need too much make-up.

AMERICAN author Gary Shteyngart was signing copies of his best-selling book *Super Sad True Love Story* at Glasgow's Aye Write! book festival when a fan put in front of him a book encased in a plastic cover.

Perhaps Gary, who signed the copy with a flourish, thought it was a fan who just took good care of his books, but a member of the Mitchell Library where the event had taken place knew better – only in Glasgow surely would someone ask an author to sign a library book.

REACTING to the latest news about celebrities using the courts to hide their lurid shenanigans, a librarian in Orkney told friends: "I think I'll spend some time crossing out random lines in celebrity biographies with black marker pen, then tell borrowers it's due to super-injunctions."

THE START of the Edinburgh Festival reminds Ninian Fergus of the old tale about the Edinburgh chap, asked about the festival, who replied that he hoped to catch Ibsen.

"*Doll's House* or *Hedda Gabler?*" he was asked. "No, Ibsen Rangers at Easter Road a week on Sunday."

READER Frank Eardley walked past a poster advertising a show by Scots comedian Frankie Boyle at Edinburgh's Festival Theatre that had "Sold Out" printed across it.

Someone had added below: "Sad but inevitable – they all do in the end."

NEIL ARTHUR on Arran heard the BBC report that "ITV has axed *Taggart* after poor viewing figures south of the Border" and thinks: "Shame that this gives away the murderer, the weapon, the victim and the motive in one sentence. In true *Taggart* tradition could they not have spun it out for an hour?"

THE NEWS reminded us of when the splendid Alex Norton, who played Inspector Matt Burke in *Taggart*, was attending a political rally

Boyzone to play gig in Inverness

BOYZONE is the latest big name band to announce a Highland date.

The original Irish boy band, which has sold over 15 records worldwide, will appear at the Northern Meeting Park in Inverness on Saturday 27th August.

Former "X Factor" winner Shane Ward will provide the support for Boyzone in front of 12,000 people at the city centre venue.

many moons ago and a wee wummin trying to flog the Communist Party's newspaper was bellowing: "*Morning Star!*"

Alex couldn't resist shouting back: "Morning missus!"

AMERICAN country band The Wilders, from Kansas City, told the audience at their Stirling gig that, as it was unseasonably warm at their recent concert at the Shetland Folk Festival, two of the band decided to take a dip in the North Sea.

"I'll tell you this," intoned frontman Ike Sheldon, "it was the quickest sex change operation in the history of mankind."

TOURING Scotland was *Italia 'n' Caledonia* by Mike Maran and Philip Contini, which tells the story of the many Italians who left sunny hillsides and emigrated to Scotland at the start of last century.

Mike tells us that the people of Lucca in Tuscany were famous for making wax figurines. Seven young statue-makers sought their fortune in Scotland and brought 1,000 little statues of the Virgin Mary all the way to Paisley – where they didn't sell.

Anyway, one of the seven, a chap called Nardini, bought the statues from his six companions who returned to Italy. Nardini set to work and converted the 1,000 Marys into 1,000 Santa Clauses, sold the lot, and opened a cafe in Largs with the profits.

THE FABULOUS Dolly Parton was appearing at Glasgow's SECC.

Fin Shearer in Newlands was shown a ticket for the event by a pal on which was printed "Dolly Parton (No support)" and naturally he couldn't stop himself from commenting: "Her back will be killing her by the end of the night."

THE EDINBURGH International Film Festival programme was launched with the Institut Français d'Ecosse as one of the venues. A receptionist at the Institut tells us that a chap once phoned and asked with some urgency if she could translate the French phrase "Frotti Frotta".

Nervously wondering where the conversation was going, she told him it meant flirting or foreplay.

"Thanks hen," replied the chap before hanging up, "that's my crossword finished."

RANDOM Edinburgh Fringe gag: "I wish I hadn't arrested a magician last night," said the policeman. "The trouble started when I asked him to empty his pockets."

CREOSOTE-TANNED Martin Cabble, a dreadful/fantastic performer on TV show *Britain's Got Talent*, appeared at the Fringe as camp cruise ship entertainer Kevin Cruise with tales of when he himself had such a job.

He reminds us of an old Diary favourite when he tells us: "You learn about the dark side of the cruise ship world. For instance, when they suddenly start serving lots of ice cream at dinner time, and everybody's standing round getting excited at all the desserts on offer at the buffet, you know it's because they've had to make room for poor Beryl who's no longer with us."

COMEDIAN Ruby Wax, performing her show, *Losing It*, along with singer Judith Owen, tells us she first appeared at the Edinburgh Festival twenty years ago, or as she put it: "I was here before the castle was built."

She also reminisced about her student days in Glasgow at the RSAMD and recalled affectionately: "I went to Glasgow before it was Starbucked to death – when it was just an ashtray with a couple of stop lights." Yes, happy days.

FOLK who care about such things were agog that Hollywood couple Brad Pitt and Angelina Jolie were in Glasgow for the filming of his zombie movie *World War Z*. Says reader Stephen Porteous in Edinburgh: "Brad and Angelina should visit the Barras while in Glasgow – as they'll be able to buy a copy of their film as soon as they've finished shooting it."

GLASGOW'S George Square was turned into Philadelphia for Brad Pitt's zombie film. A reader claimed that in homage to Glasgow's younger citizens, Brad is considering renaming the film *The Night of the Living Ned*.

RANDOM Fringe joke: "My job is testing theatre trapdoors.

"It's a stage I'm going through."

AUTHOR Janice Galloway, appearing at Edinburgh Book Festival, was reminded by event host Ruth Wishart of the advice Janice's granny gave Janice when she was growing up in the Ayrshire seaside resort of Saltcoats.

The old lady would warn her: "Don't go near the Glasgow folk Janice, they're on their holidays. Anything could happen."

RADIO 1 DJ Tom Deacon, whose Edinburgh Fringe show, *Can I Be Honest?*, was at the Pleasance Dome, had been flying back to London every week to record his radio show.

Returning to Edinburgh after the London riots, Tom was told by his taxi driver at Edinburgh airport who heard his accent: "Well pal, I bet you didnae think you'd feel safer in Scotland."

GLAMOROUS Glasgow jazz trio, the Swingcats, recently met the lighting engineer of one of Britain's biggest rock bands on a plane. He told them that one of the big stars in the band always carries a piece with him wherever he goes.

Says Swingcat Alyson Orr: "We told him that we carried pieces everywhere as well, as you're never sure what the airline food is going to be like. We got quite excited about a world-famous rock star carrying a packed lunch until the engineer quietly pointed out he meant a gun, not tuna and sweetcorn."

THE OSCARS were being discussed on the bus into Glasgow, where one chap declared: "I don't get a gold statue for being good at my job, so why should they?"

RANDOM Edinburgh Fringe gag: "My friend said he would give me a tenner if I did a bungee jump.

"But I wasn't falling for that."

THE TROUBLED life of American actor Charlie Sheen was in the news. A reader sees the headline on one news website "Sacked Sheen Sues Show", and wonders: "By the seashore?"

BUSY Scots author Des Dillon not only has a new novel out, *An Experiment in Compassion*, but he also did stand-up at Glasgow's Tron Theatre where a fellow Coatbridge resident in the audience described her pal as a posh ned.

"She drinks Buckfast and talks posh," the girl explained.

"A posh Buckie drinker?" said Des.

"Aye, she drinks it out of a cup at work so's her boss doesn't see her," she continued.

"Where does she work?" asked Des.

"A care home."

Needless to say the Glasgow audience thought this was hilarious.

A REGULAR visitor to Glasgow is quiz show host Anne Robinson, whose programme is recorded by BBC Scotland. A young chap who saw her get out of a taxi in the West End the other day tells us: "I put some body spray on last night, but I only managed to pull Anne Robinson.

"It must have been the weakest Lynx."

AMERICAN singer-songwriter Ryan Adams infuriated fans at a Glasgow gig by talking incoherently at great length between numbers.

Iain McGregor, who was there that night, tells us: "Someone shouted out, 'Hurry up! I've to get to my work in the morning.'"

COMEDIAN Peter Kay's show at Glasgow's SECC sold out nearly two years in advance.

A Newton Mearns reader bought tickets at the time not realising the show was not until 2011.

When the ticket office worker pointed this out, our reader replied: "Two years? I could be dead by then."

"Peter Kay could be dead by then," replied the helpful ticket seller.

SINGER Darius Campbell was the handsome hunk prince at the King's panto in Glasgow. As he turned to the audience and told them he would search all over the world for his missing Snow White, a woman in the circle couldn't contain herself, and shouted out: "I'm up here!"

OUR TALE of the Australian jackeroo shooting the cinema screen reminds author Les Brown of seeing the film *Jaws* in New York when the haunting soundtrack indicated that the shark was approaching children swimming.

The chap sitting in front of Les jumped up and shouted: "Get out the water! Can you no' hear the shark music?"

CINEMA interruptions, continued. Mike Fagan saw *Braveheart* in Kilmarnock, which began, of course, with the sombre killings of Scots by the English king, Edward Longshanks.

That was before the dramatic fightback, where the Scots under Wallace raise long pikes in front of the charging English cavalry, leading to the slaughter of both horses and riders. There was a massive cheer in the cinema with a chap in the back shouting out: "Aye, youse lot, this wan's no goin' tae penalties!"

ROBERT MURPHY, scriptwriter on the Stephen Tompkinson television series *DCI Banks*, knew he was back in Glasgow when he asked a shop assistant what forms of payment he could make.

"We accept," said the assistant, "everything apart from American Express, and ginger bottles."

PANTO dame Johnny McKnight was reading out the birthdays at *Snow White* at Stirling's MacRobert Centre when a girl in the very back row jumped up and down when he announced her name.

Spotting her at the back, Johnny remarked: "Maybe for your ninth birthday, your parents will book earlier so you can see."

AND AN actor who played the panto baddie in Glasgow some years ago says his favourite pantomime joke came in *Robinson Crusoe* at the King's, when Rikki Fulton as the dame turned to Larry Marshall and declared: "Jings! Mah feet are killin' me."

"Whit's wrang wi yer feet?" enquired Larry.

"Sciatica," said Rikki.

"Hoo can ye ha' sciatica in yer feet?" asked Larry.

"Well, these shoes are size six, an' see ah take a seven."

"I'M SURPRISED Colin Firth was up for an Oscar for his role in *The King's Speech*," said the chap in the pub the other night. "I've just seen the film, and Firth stumbled over most of his lines."

RAGTIME blues band Pokey LaFarge & The South City Three, appearing at the Acoustic Music Centre during the Fringe, were recently interviewed on BBC Radio Devon. Asked what they were doing after their show, they said they would be cooking a "four-pint chicken dish" which their manager from Paisley had shown them.

When asked for the recipe, St Louis-born Pokey replied: "You throw the chicken in the pan with some potatoes, carrots, onions and stock. Then go out to the pub for four pints. When you return, it's ready."

TAURUS APRIL 21 - MAY 21

There will be much activity taking place behind the scenes for you this year and over the next seven years as you develop new ideas. What you are doing is preparing foundations and building yourself a solid core for the future.

Although it's not like you to daydream you will now find yourself drifting off into reveries. Don't stop this, allow your mind to go into free fall because that is what will give your subconscious time to work and to come up with those amazing flashes of inspiration.

If you wonder where all those bright ideas, inventions and intuitive insights are coming from, it's Uranus.

Your dreams are also likely to be more colourful and in some cases prophetic. Listen to your intuition and follow through but beware of nervous strain and take extra care of your legs. Poor footwear could lead to pulled muscles and sprains.

WHILE in Glasgow for a show at Hampden Park, Sir Paul McCartney was jogging through Glasgow Green when he called in at the Winter Gardens for a cuppa.

When he said "Hello Samantha" to one of the Encore catering ladies – fortunately he didn't actually burst into singing the Cliff Richard song – the star-struck lady asked how he knew her name.

"I'm a qualified clairvoyant," Paul replied – then pointed at her name badge.

ALISTAIR SLOAN in Ayr was at the Jim Bowen show at the Fringe where an Edinburgh girl was asked in the general knowledge part of the game show: "Which old Queen was retired to Long Beach, California?" She answered: "Liberace."

A LETTER in *The Herald* suggesting that comedian Billy Connolly should have worn a tie to receive the freedom of the city reminds us when Diary pal Russell Kyle accompanied Billy to Celtic Park, where they were receiving hospitality as guests of then Celtic owner Fergus McCann.

Just as they were about to meet Fergus, Russell realised Billy was tie-less and, as Fergus was a stickler for the convention that guests should wear shirts and ties, Russell quickly whispered to Billy that Fergus might say something.

Instead, Billy strode forward, shook Fergus's hand and told him: "What kind of club is this you're running? I've only been here twenty minutes and already someone's nicked ma tie."

A GOLF club philosopher asks us: "Why do the folk who get kicked off of *The X Factor* always say that this isn't the last you'll see of them?

As I've no intention of holidaying at Butlin's, I'm pretty sure it is."

CONGRATULATIONS to Paisley's Paolo Nutini for winning best male singer in the Q Awards. When a local in a Paisley pub yesterday asked: "Did you hear who won the Q Awards?" someone piped up: "Elderslie Post Office on pensions' day?"

A TABLOID newspaper reported that American rock band Kings of Leon want to play an open-air gig in Glasgow's Bellahouston Park. An American reader tells us the band abandoned a concert in St Louis this summer as pigeons defecated on them. Bass player Jared Followill, interviewed on CNN, couldn't say how many birds there were, and added: "The last thing I was going to do was look up."

GLASGOW'S West End Festival included an acoustic music evening in memory of Allan Mawn, the West End restaurateur who tragically died.

We remember that before Allan opened Velvet Elvis and Pintxo restaurants, he was entertainments boss at Strathclyde Students Union where he hired the amiable panto-performing Krankies to do an adult-themed show for the students.

Janette, in her persona as Wee Jimmy Krankie, nodded at husband Ian and announced: "How sick is he? He likes his wife to dress up as a wee schoolboy."

MISHEARD song lyrics occupied the minds of readers. "My mother was not at all surprised that Lucille left Kenny Rogers with '400 children and a crop in the field'," says Ian Beattie.

JOHN ARMSTRONG in Dundee says: "Lucille? I always thought Kenny Rogers was complaining about a footwear malfunction, probably when he was running for a bus. 'You picked a fine time to leave me, loose heel!'"

SAYS Iain McGregor: "Every time I hear Creedence Clearwater Revival singing 'Bad Moon Rising' I always think they are singing, 'There's a bathroom on the right.' Perhaps it's something to do with being an architect."

SAYS Alistair Hems: "I always thought Elvis had a problem with the child that was born on a cold and grey Chicago morning being brought up in the gateaux."

ELISA YOUNG hears Rihanna singing her latest hit S&M with the chorus: "Whips and chains excite me," and wonders if young Ayrshire women sing: "Chips and weans excite me," instead.

6.
The Shopping Experience

More Scots than ever are of course buying goods online. But you just don't get the same rapport as when you venture out into the stores, as these stories prove.

SKIN treatment clinic Destination Skin has recently opened in Frasers in Glasgow. One of the staff tells us about treating a lady and asking her what her makeup removal routine was in the evening. The lady simply replied: "Pillow."

JUDE HUNTER was in Primark in Glasgow when the girls behind him in the queue were talking about dogs, and asked him if he had any.

He told them he had two mini dachshunds, but that didn't seem to register with the girls, as one asked: "Is that like a greyhound?" So Jude explained that they were also popularly known as sausage dogs.

"What, square?" asked the bemused girl.

A SHOPKEEPER phones to tell us about the latest must-have toy for Christmas. "Nintendo has brought out a game where you run after a ten-year-old boy on your TV screen around the streets of Glasgow after he has smashed a window of your car.

"It's called the Wii Bastirt."

AN ELDERLY reader getting her prescription in Partick tells us the girl in front of her asked the assistant for a pregnancy testing kit. The assistant pointed to two or three different makes and asked which type she would like.

"A negative one, please," the girl replied.

PET FOOD company Whiskas sells Cat Milk for owners who know that ordinary cows' milk can upset their pets' stomachs. A reader in a Newton Mearns supermarket watched the young girl in front of him point at it and tell her friend: "Look. Cat Milk."

"That's disgusting. Milking the wee things," replied her perplexed pal.

A READER'S failure to find sparkling water at a Paisley burger van reminds Allan Boyd in Clarkston of a colleague being told by his wife to pick up a star fruit on the way home for a dinner party.

Says Allan: "As he was driving through Bridgeton, he spied a fruiterer's and pulled over.

"He asked the wee wummin serving him if she had a star fruit. She looked at him for a minute, then said, 'A star fruit? Listen son, this is Brigton. We only got bananas here two years ago.'"

OUR TALES of being unable to find exotic fruit and veg in certain parts of Scotland reminds Angus Black of the valuable advice his wife was given when trying to buy kumquats in Paisley. The fruit shop did not stock them, and the fruiterer explained: "Kumquats! Hen, this is Paisley. If they cannae spell it, they'll no eat it."

A BEARSDEN reader heard his daughter announce, "That's disgusting!" while filling out her online shopping order with Sainsbury's. When he inquired what had agitated her she pointed out the webpage for toilet rolls listed for each brand "cost per sht".

"It's just an abbreviation for sheet," he reassured her.

SPOTTED in Tesco, Springburn, by Carmen Wood – a large display of Scottish goods at the end of one aisle including shortbread, oatmeal and haggis, plus Chinese curry powder. When Carmen queried why it was in a Scottish display, an assistant explained: "Look at the packaging. It's manufactured in Coatbridge."

A READER shopping at a Sauchiehall Street store heard an alarm go off at the door where a woman just leaving stopped as she wondered if she had set it off.

A security guard asked her: "Have you bought something in another store? Primark perhaps?"

"How dare you," the woman replied.

STEPHEN DOYLE visited a Chinese supermarket in Swansea, where he spent a while buying some spices, noodles and one or two large pieces of hardware.

As he was paying at the till, the man behind the counter took a look at what Stephen had bought and said: "Do you have a wok?"

"No," said Stephen, "the car is just across the road."

READER Charlie Bell was in a Dunoon charity shop where he was admiring a miniature model of the famous Liberty Bell in Philadelphia, complete with its equally famous fissure. When he asked the lady in the shop how much it was she said: "A pound."

Then after looking at it further, she added: "Sorry son, it's got a crack in it. I'll only charge you 50p."

A READER swears he was in a Glasgow Asda where an old chap using the self-service checkout couldn't find the right bit to press to have his bag of potatoes weighed. A member of staff, seeing his dilemma, went over, found the right spot, pressed it, and told him: "The vegetables are listed alphabetically. P for potatoes."

"Ah, I was lookin under T for tatties, son," the old fella replied.

WE MENTIONED the senior citizen in Asda trying to look up potatoes on the self-scanner under T "for tatties". A Hyndland reader reckons many old guys in supermarkets just like a laugh to keep themselves going. He saw one chap with his wife buying a large bag of ice cubes, presumably for a party, and the old fella turned to the bemused checkout girl and asked: "Now are these fresh? I don't like buying the frozen rubbish."

JIM LAUGHLAN in Fife went into his local convenience store where he asked if they had any Bird's Custard. The look of puzzlement on the assistant's face finally disappeared when he asked Jim: "Do you mean Trill?"

GOOD to see the healthy living message is finally hitting home in Glasgow. Suzanne Wards was waiting for a prescription at her local chemist when a chap with a heroin addiction – in common parlance, a junkie – came in.

"You in for your methadone?" asked the pharmacist, referring to the commonly prescribed heroin substitute.

"Aye," the chap replied, before adding: "Mind, mine's sugar-free."

"I'M SLEEPING on the couch again tonight," announced the chap in the pub.

After one or two mutterings of sympathy from his fellow topers, he then added: "I have to tell you, it's great being the night watchman at the DFS showroom."

GREGGS, the fast-food chain much favoured by Glaswegians, has been told to change the name of its big selling Cornish Pasties as under EU law the name can now only refer to such delicacies made in Cornwall. Greggs is asking customers what to rename them, with the favourite being "the pasty formerly known as Cornish".

However, as many people dispute the Greggs offering is anything like the real thing, we prefer the suggestion "Cornish Pastiche".

WE'VE mentioned the tanks of garra rufa fish at Glasgow's Silverburn shopping centre where weary shoppers plunk their feet in to have a soothing massage from the tiny fish nibbling at their hard skin.

Carol Foote, who was there the other day, tells us: "As I went over to take a look at the fish, a couple in their late sixties came walking up purposefully. The woman had her purse out – obviously intending to have a wee dip of her tootsies. Before she could say anything to the assistant, the husband said in a loud voice, 'Can she have the tank with the piranhas?'"

A WEST END socialite saw her local dry cleaners had a three for two offer on cleaning dresses and took a few along. Unfortunately, the small print said it did not apply to evening dresses, and she and the cleaning assistant got into an argument about what constituted an evening dress.

As the assistant said her dresses did not qualify for the special offer as they looked like evening dresses, our reader indignantly asked how the assistant would define what dresses the offer applied to.

In a convincing example of Glasgow logic, the assistant replied: "Dresses you would wear to Asda."

ANNIE McQUISTON, in the snowy wasteland of Glasgow's south side during the worst of the winter weather, heard a woman coming out of a corner shop declaring: "I'm on the snow diet. Nae breid!"

A READER claims he was in his corner shop when a fellow customer picked up a bag of coffee, peered at it, then asked: "When is this 'best before'?" The shopkeeper replied: "Well, for me, it's best before coming to work in the morning."

CAROL KNIGHT tells us that a neighbour in Partick was Christmas shopping and trying to find a T-shirt of the American rap artist Lil Wayne for her teenage son, but drew a blank.

As she passed a skate shop, her eleven-year-old daughter suggested they try in there, so she went in with her daughter and asked: "Do you have a Lil Wayne T-shirt?"

"No, they start at adult sizes," said the assistant.

GORDON PHILLIPS tells us about a regular in the Chestnuts Hotel in Ayr explaining that he was given a demonstration of a 3D television when he visited an electrical store, and was handed a pair of 3D glasses by the assistant.

When the assistant came back to ask him what he thought of it, the chap said no way was he prepared to sit just two feet away from the telly.

It was then gently explained to him that he could watch from a lot further back, once the security chain had been removed from the specs.

THE PROBLEMS of delivery drivers on the frozen roads of Scotland reminded a Paisley reader of when he ran a shop in the town, and a German delivery driver came in to ask for directions to Clydebank. "For goodness sake, son," said the customer behind him, "your faither found it easily enough in the dark."

CHRISTMAS sales buying can be a fraught business in miserable weather. One frustrated chap was heard explaining his annoyance at trekking around the shops to his girlfriend: "So how would you like it if I took you into eight pubs one after the other and didn't buy you a drink in any of them, before finally going back to the first one we were in and getting a drink there?"

AND A shopper heading to Silverburn on Glasgow's south side claimed: "I was stuck in traffic for so long even the sat nav was asking, 'Are we nearly there yet?'"

A READER sees the BBC headline "Swine flu vaccine stock released" and tells us: "I don't know about you, but I think I'll just stick to my usual beef or vegetable ones."

AFTER our story about the B&Q customer bamboozling the Polish member of staff by asking for "a hing tae hing hings oan" readers recall other such feats of linguistics.

There was the foreign tourist asking for the bus to Ayr at Buchanan Bus Station and the driver pointing to another stance and replying: "'Err Ayr ower err."

And of course the customer in Aberdeen buying ski boots and not being sure which was the left and right one. Or, as she asked: "Fit fits fit fit?"

A SALES assistant in a Glasgow fashion store tells us of the best riposte she has heard when an undecided customer came out of the changing rooms in a dress she had tried on, and asked her waiting partner: "Does this dress make me look fat?" He thought about this for a moment before replying: "Does this tie make me look stupid?"

IT'S NOT just Scottish accents that can be puzzling. Duncan Bradon tells us his Lancastrian daughter-in-law was in a Borders supermarket where, wishing to freshen her mouth, she asked a member of staff where she might find some mints.

"Fresh or frozen?" he asked.

BEFORE Valentine's Day, Hugh Paton was much taken with the card on sale in Morrison's which showed a little boy, dressed as a grown-up, carrying a rose and leaning forward to kiss a little girl. Above them the card stated: "For The One I Love".

And on top of that was a sticker stating: "Buy One. Get One Free".

DO WOMEN think differently from men? We only ask as Andy Cumming tells us that his wife returned home to say she was walking through Glasgow's Royal Exchange Square when she saw a miscreant running out of a handbag shop with half-a-dozen handbags while a shop assistant gave chase.

"Could you give a description?" asked Andy, wondering if his wife should do her civic duty and come forward as a witness.

"Well, there were two big black ones, a nice tan one, a small red one, and a nice yellow one," she replied.

A READER out shopping in Drumchapel heard a woman in the supermarket ask her friend if she used the self-service checkout tills.

"Use them?" replied her pal. "I use them so much I'm surprised I wasn't named employee of the month in January."

A READER swears he was in a south-side chemist's when a chap came in and asked the pharmacist if he had anything for hiccups.

Without warning, the pharmacist reached over and smacked the man between the shoulder blades and asked: "Did that help?"

"I doubt it," the customer replied. "But if you like I'll go and check with my wife who is waiting out in the car."

A GLASGOW reader in a city centre card shop watched as an old timer holding a fancy large card bent down to work out from the list of codes how much it cost. He looked surprised, as we often do at the price of a piece of cardboard, then muttered to no-one in particular: "If I'd wanted to spend that much, I'd have bought her a present, no' a card."

A READER heard a woman having coffee with friends in the Newton Mearns shopping centre declare that her husband so rarely helped her do the shopping that when he entered the supermarket the other day, the machine automatically announced: "Unexpected item in the bagging area."

AN EAST KILBRIDE reader tells us her son-in-law was at the supermarket with his two-year-old twins when a fellow shopper, seeing the twins, rather wittily said to him: "Was it buy one, get one free?"

Unfortunately, son-in-law, thinking the shopper was referring to the cases of beer in his trolley, confusingly replied: "No, they're £6 each – but there are shelves full of them."

LINGERIE and beauty boutique Odyssey recently opened in Edinburgh with the stock including a range of discreet, em, electronic massagers for the ladies. Odyssey owner Sarah Connelly had to watch as her dad picked up one of the toys, started shaking it, and asked: "How do you get it to start playing the music?"

GLASGOW public relations worker Claire Cook popped into a fancy-dress shop in Rutherglen in preparation for her fortieth birthday party. A chap in his fifties came in behind her and asked the assistant for a *Shrek* outfit.

The young girl started showing the chap a naughty nurse's uniform, followed by a saucy French maid's outfit. As the customer's face turned a deep red, the assistant suddenly stopped and said: "Oh, you asked me for a *Shrek* outfit, didn't you? Not a sex outfit."

A READER feels the most ironic thing he has seen was the chap in an East End of Glasgow Asda store at the weekend who bought forty fags and a bottle of vodka . . . and then produced a "Bag for Life" to put them in.

A RENFREWSHIRE reader swears he was in his local supermarket when the check-out girl asked the pensioner in front of him: "Would you like help with your packing?" and the auld fella replied: "That would be great — but how did you know I was going on holiday?"

7.
Drinking In Moderation

Scotland's bars are under pressure from rising prices and the smoking ban. Hopefully some of these stories will remind people why a pint and a blether are still a good thing.

GLASGOW barmen – amongst the best in the world, we reckon. Scott Barclay in Hamilton tells us about friends John and Claire visiting from Colorado who popped in to Glasgow's esteemed Horseshoe Bar, where Claire asked for a gin and Slimline tonic.

The barman looked at his shelves before telling her: "We only have full-fat, hen. Away and run round the block, and I'll watch your drink."

A TOPER in the Highlands tells us the locals have nicknamed their local pub the Moderation.

That way they can all tell their doctors that they only drink in moderation.

KENNY REID was watching *Horizon* on the telly and noted that one of the scientists on the programme was called Beau Lotto, and thought to himself: "Surely that's what much of Scotland gets on a Friday night?"

A LANARKSHIRE reader tells us there is an old fella in his local pub every day doing his newspaper crossword. Unwary newcomers occasionally ask if he needs any help. Invariably he replies: "Four letter word, beginning with 'P', a measurement of liquid."

"Pint?" replies the visitor.

"Thanks, I'll have a Tennent's," the pensioner tells them.

SAYS Rod Macdonald: "When I first came to Glasgow I was having a drink in the Park Bar with two friends. One of them insisted that we go to the Pot Still because they had hundreds of different bottles of whisky. He eventually persuaded us to get a taxi there, and I had a pint of lager, my other mate had a vodka and he had a Bacardi and coke."

BILL McMILLAN of Linlithgow tells us: "The landlord of a pub beside a well-known Glasgow dog track told me that race nights were his busiest evenings when the pub was full with punters and dog-owners with their dugs. On one evening the door opened and a regular whom he had previously barred asked if the ban was still in place. When he was told it was, his reaction to the unwelcome news was to tip out three live rabbits he was carrying in a bag into the centre of the pub and make a hasty retreat."

THE REDOUBTABLE entertainer Andy Cameron tells us, and who are we to doubt him: "A blonde brassy barmaid in Maryhill was stunned at the good looks of a tall handsome stranger who walked in, and as she served him his pint she says, 'Hivnae seen you in here afore – jist moved intae the area like?'

"'No,' says the tall fella, 'I live round the corner, but I've been away for twenty years and I've just come back.'

"'Oh,' she giggles, 'a merchant seaman are you?'

"'No, I've been in prison for murdering my wife and her mother.'

"The stunned silence round the bar was only broken by the barmaid asking, 'Oh, on yer own then?'"

AND AN honourable mention to Frank O'Donnell in Fife, who recounts: "A local character in Auchterarder ordered a hawf and a hawf, announcing to the barman that he was sixty-two today.

"The barman said, 'Have that one on me.' Thanking the barman for his generosity, he then proceeded to inform the bar that next week he was two to ten."

HELEN MAXWELL tells us: "The George Hotel in Moniaive is very old and the public bar has flagstones on the floor.

"Years ago when an inspector came from health and hygiene, he asked if the owner was going to cover the floor.

"The proprietor said yes, and when asked what with, he replied, 'Customers' feet.'"

EWEN BAIRD tells us that when the Royal Bar in Helensburgh installed 3D television, they charged punters a £2 deposit on the special glasses. The Imperial Hotel further up the road also went for the 3D option and charged a £5 deposit.

Says Ewen: "The initiative of the locals was ably demonstrated when the owner of the Imperial was surprised to have twice the number of glasses returned, while the owner of the Royal was left wondering why none were returned to him. A pricing agreement was later made between the two pubs."

ALAN BARLOW in Paisley tells us about a local pub used by players from the nearby bingo hall. One of the ladies took unwell and muttered: "It's all the pills I've taken."

She was taken to hospital where, to be safe, her stomach was pumped. It was only after, says Alan, that she came round and explained: "No' they kind of pills. It's the Pils lager."

GORDON at the George Hotel in Inveraray tells us about a labourer over at Loch Awe who liked a dram before going home for his tea. He had just polished off a plate of mince 'n' tatties and a large glass of milk his wife had placed before him after a trip to the pub when the police arrived and breathalysed him following a tip-off he had been driving erratically.

He just scraped through the test and told the cops: "Well it's either the milk or the mince which is great at neutralising the alcohol," before his face darkened and he added, "Unless that sod at the pub is watering the vodka."

A LANARKSHIRE reader hears a bold lad in his local tell a young woman to whom he was chatting that he was from "the US of A".

Our reader was just thinking that the lad's accent did not sound in the least transatlantic, when the chap then added for clarification: "The underside of Airdrie."

ONLY in Glasgow. Barman Mark Ross, working in a hotel on the outskirts of the city, had to tell a tipsy customer attending a birthday bash that he could no longer serve her as it was after hours.

Not giving up easily she then asked: "Can ye no just gee me a wee glass ae wine? Ye know, like a kid's portion o' wine?"

YOU CAN'T beat a Scottish education. Bernard Henderson was in a Kirkcaldy pub on a karaoke night when a lady was belting out Carly Simon's "You're So Vain". As the words came up on screen she sang the line: "You had me several years ago when I was still quite naive," but pronounced it as "knave".

Realising that was wrong she shouted at the chap running the show: "Billy, your machine cannae spell."

ADAM, the barman in the Lismore in the West End of Glasgow, watched as two punters compared their new mobile phones. One whipped out a BlackBerry and said he'd downloaded an application that e-mails you when your football team scored.

"That's brilliant," replied his pal. "Does it work?"

"Nae idea," replied the BlackBerry owner. "I'm a Partick Thistle fan."

RON WILLIAMSON reminded us of the classic tale of the barmaid trying to pour a customer a pint of Maclays, but the barrel needed changed.

When she shouted at the charge-hand: "That's Maclays aff!" the customer naturally replied: "Wait a minute – I hardly know you."

A BBC contact was sipping champagne cocktails in Glasgow's Rogano last week when she heard a chap ask about a table for lunch, but was told by the maître d' that it would be a bit of a wait as there were only two empty tables and both were reserved.

The chap looked around, did a quick count, and told the maître d': "I can see a few empty tables – what about those?" as he pointed over towards the back of the restaurant.

"You're looking in the mirror sir," the member of staff quietly replied.

A READER claims he was in a smart Glasgow bar before Christmas when a chap drained his whisky and announced: "Got to get to the office party. To tell you the truth, I can't stand any of them who'll be there – a real bunch of crawlers."

When the barman asked him why he bothered going, the toper replied: "I'm the boss, it's expected of me."

A CHAP who had not been in the pub for a while explained his absence: "I broke my leg and the doc said he was going to put me in a cast."

He then added: "How he expected me to sing and dance in that condition I'll never know."

FESTIVE time in the pubs and, in one giant bar in Glasgow, a young chap was heard telling a young woman he was a "marine coating and heating engineer". He never got round to explaining he actually fried fish in the Blue Lagoon chip shop.

"MY DOCTOR has just discovered I'm colour blind," said the chap in the pub.

"It was a real bolt out of the red."

PUBS are famed of course for their amateur comedians. "I bought ma wee niece a torch for her birthday," one chap declared in the pub the other day.

"You should have seen her wee face light up."

STEPHEN THOMAS witnessed an argument in a Glasgow pub over the merits of buying someone a non-alcoholic drink. As the chap declared with perfect logic: "Naw, you're no' gettin' another Coke. If you were sitting in the house you wouldnae have three Cokes in a row, would ye?"

"I GOT aroused watching *Countdown* the other night," said the loud-mouth in the pub.

"Not bad – seven letters," he added.

JIM HAIR in Dalry was at a pub quiz where a contestant was asked to name a fish beginning with C.

"Chuna," the chap replied.

OUR STORY of sandwich fillings reminds Bill McEwan of when he was teaching physics in Motherwell.

Says Bill: "I was discussing the main components of a radio and was attempting to elucidate the function of the tuner when I noticed a look of confusion on one pupil's face.

"When I asked if he had a problem, he said that he didn't understand why a radio needed a fish."

READER Nick Austwick was in one of the more challenging pubs in Cambuslang and asked his companion if they would be safe there. "Just don't show them your teeth," he replied. "They hate folk with teeth."

DOUGIE McNICOL in Bridge of Weir heard two chaps in the pub discussing a football-loving friend who was in hospital. "So, it looks like he's gonny miss a' the European gemmes," opined one.

"He'll be able tae see them on Sky," replied his pal.

But the first chap disagreed. "It's the hospital he's in – no' the jail."

NOT THE best chat-up line, we reckon, from the chap a reader over-heard in a Glasgow city-centre pub at the weekend. He approached a girl, out with her pals, who was wearing a tiara which said "Birthday Girl". "How old are you?" he asked.

"Pushing thirty," the woman giggled.

"From which direction?" he replied.

A READER overhears a group of lads in a large Glasgow pub working out what they are going to drink. "It's three pounds a pint, or a pitcher for a tenner," said one.

"Why would I want my photo taken drinking lager?" asked his pal.

8.
Nostalgia

Nostalgia, as someone once observed, is a thing of the past. Here are some of our readers' favourite memories.

IT WAS forty years ago that decimalisation was introduced, with many programmes on telly explaining the changeover, and shops sneakily putting up their prices hoping we wouldn't notice. As one auld biddy declared in a butcher's shop at the time: "I can't understand why the Government didn't just wait until all the old folk had died before bringing in this new-fangled money."

MIKE ELLIOTT in Glasgow was an eighteen-year-old working in a Leeds pub then. He recalls: "I remember being sorely tempted to help myself to generous tips when inebriated or frustrated customers would empty their pockets of change on to the counter and say, 'I can't work out this toy money son, just you take the correct amount.'

"Happy days."

WE ASKED for your "auld money" stories to mark the anniversary of decimalisation, and Jim Scott in Singapore recalls: "When I was about six, we lived on the top floor of a tenement in Tobago Street, and my gran lived in London Road near Glasgow Cross.

"One day I fell out with my dad, and decided I was going to stay with my gran. So I packed my bag, went all the way down four flights of stairs, out onto the street, when my dad shouted on me from the top floor to come back.

"I thought he was going to give in to whatever it was I was after, so I went all the way back up the stairs only to meet my dad at the door, who handed me half-a-crown and said, 'Give that to your gran for your keep.'"

AULD money continued. A reader tells us about a shop in Kirkintilloch, days after decimalisation, where a sympathetic shop assistant asked an old customer: "How are you managing with this new money?" The auld fella replied: "Aw it'll no catch oan in Kirkintilloch."

AND COMEDIAN Stu Who reminds us that changing the currency has meant many popular phrases were no longer in use. He adds: "Who can forget the legendary, 'He's getting right oan ma thruppennies!'" If you don't understand that one, ask an auld yin.

REMINISCING about boozy business lunches reminds Gordon Kerr in Stroud: "Back in the 1970s a friend took a rough-and-ready, but extremely rich, builder to lunch at the old Malmaison. When the wine waiter arrived the guest said, 'A pint of heavy son,' but was told they did not serve beer.

"Spying The Toby Jug pub across the road, the builder pulled out a fiver and said, 'They do – just keep bringing them.' The waiter didn't bat an eyelid and, bearing in mind it was about 32p a pint then, the tailed waiter crossed with a pint of McEwans on a silver tray every thirty minutes or so."

WE ASKED for your memories of the boozy business lunches, and John Crawford tell us: "Many years ago my mate sold refuse collection vehicles, and had to entertain a leftwing council leader to lunch after receiving a good order. On being offered the wine list, the councillor chose a bottle each of the most expensive red and white wines, poured himself half a glass of each, then shouted, 'Corks.'

"The waiters, obviously used to this, brought him the corks, which he forced into the bottles, stuck one in each jacket pocket then ordered two pints of lager."

WE REMINISCED about the boozy business lunches, and John Gilligan tells us of Big John who covered the south side of Glasgow for Dryburghs the brewers in the late 1960s. He recalls: "One day John was accompanied by a senior manager from England who, after his eighth call to licensed premises, and the eighth alcoholic beverage, asked John, 'Do you always drink this much during the day?'

"Big John replied, 'Naw, some days we go fur a bevy.'"

OUR REMINISCING reminds an Ayrshire reader of when his late father, a transport manager with the National Coal Board, was invited with colleagues to the Scottish Motor Show at the Kelvin Hall in the 1960s.

Company reps took them for lunch, then various hospitality events.

Says our reader: "Later that evening, I turned up to collect the old man from the St Enoch Hotel, where an engine manufacturing company had been hosting a reception.

"I arrived to find the Coal Board gang being escorted out, and the old man assuring the commissionaire, 'We have been asked to leave better hotels than this my good man. Last month in London we were invited to leave the Savoy."'

WE ASKED for your memories of the Glasgow Garden Festival and Pat Davis recalls: "As a musician in the 1980s, I had the privilege of knowing some of the most skilled work dodgers on the planet. One guy, who busked on the violin outside bingo halls, was already in his mid-thirties and had never had a 'proper' job.

"As Thatcherism bit, he was called to the dole office regularly, where he insisted that the only suitable position would be as first violinist in a concert orchestra. Then one day the weary dole officer simply smiled and handed him a card with an address where he was told to report.

"I didn't see him for some months before visiting the Garden Festival. On entering the catering hall, I was amazed to see our man for the first time ever in a suit and black tie, sitting in the front row of the band and sawing his fiddle in a completely scunnered manner, having to cope with six months of gainful employment."

GLASGOW Garden Festival continued. Airdrie lawyer Frank Nicol recalls that his then student son had a temporary job on the trams running at the festival.

At the same time Frank received an invitation to a pretentious Glasgow West End party where a posh lady asked Frank what his son did for a living. "He's a conductor," replied Frank.

"Has he ever met Andre Previn?" she gushed.

OUR STORIES about airplane seating arrangements remind Wendy Hunter in San Francisco: "I worked for the now defunct Highland Express Airlines at Prestwick. After seating was completed in a full economy class, my colleague noticed a poor wee man doing his best to get comfortable while being squashed and unable to use his armrest due to a hugely overweight woman in the seat next to him.

"My well-meaning colleague discreetly told him there was a spare seat in first class and would he like to move to it. The passenger replied that, no, he would just stay next to his wife."

TALKING of anniversaries, sadly it is fifty years since England beat Scotland 9-3 at Wembley. Years later player Bobby Shearer of Rangers was able to joke: "England cheated. They used an orange ball which goalie Frank Haffey of Celtic refused to go near, and which neither Eric Caldow nor I would kick."

GLASGOW Garden Festival continued. The festival introduced Glaswegians to foreign influences. David Green recalls: "I was with a few friends in the pub on the festival site. My mate George sees a sign stating 'Frankfurters £1'. So he then goes up to the bar and asks for a pint of Frankfurters."

TIME to end our Garden Festival tales with reader Ian Clark reminding us of the time of the festival closing, and the city looking forward to the next big thing, the European City of Culture. On the wall of the now disused Garden Festival site, someone had spray-painted: "F*** the Garden Festival. I'm off to the theatre."

WE ASKED for your Scottish wedding stories, and Stuart Miller tells us of a wedding in one of Scotland's more magnificent churches where the staff announced that there had been a mix-up, the organist had been double booked and couldn't come, but there was a piano if anyone could play it.

Eventually the couple went up the aisle to an older woman amongst the guests who could play the only religious song she knew, "Stand Up, Stand Up for Jesus", with two fingers.

"The magnificence was muted," says Stuart.

SCOTTISH weddings, and Richard Gault tells us: "When I had a July wedding in Airdrie, we walked the short distance to the hotel from the church just as the Orange March was coming up the street.

"My brother-in-law told my granny from Lossiemouth, where they don't have such things, that because I was so popular, the town band came out for my wedding. I never did find out if she ever learned the truth."

TALKING of Airdrie, local chap Patrick Rolink, doing a stand-up turn at a fundraiser for George Galloway's Coalition Against the Cuts in Glasgow, said his grandfather had been a lifelong Airdrie supporter, and when he died, the family scattered his ashes over the pitch's centre circle.

"The ground was later sold and Safeways built a supermarket on it," added Patrick. "We do get some funny looks when we go back every year and leave flowers beside the fish counter."

INCIDENTALLY, Patrick is one of the fuller-figure comedians on the circuit. He says that when he goes to an airport and they ask if he is carrying anything he shouldn't, he tells them: "Seven-and-a-half stones, but why remind me?"

WE ASKED for your Scottish wedding tales, and Gavin Paterson recounts: "Playing in a wedding band for over twenty-five years, I remember being on stage in an East End of Glasgow hall when a huge fight broke out on the dance floor.

"Word had spread that the best man had been caught in an intimate moment with the newly-married bride.

"The father of the bride came to the microphone to quell the fight by announcing, 'Right, stop the fighting. The best man has apologised.' It worked too."

AULD money continued. John MacDonald in Dubai returned to Scotland a couple of years after decimalisation and was shocked, after puffing on duty free, to see the price of a packet of fags in the pub's cigarette machine was a new-fangled 50p piece.

Says John: "I protested indignantly to the barman that I'd been ripped off – ten bob for a packet of fags. Half-a-crown was the going rate, maybe four shillings allowing for the time I'd been away, moan moan.

"The barman listened patiently to my rant, raised an eyebrow, and asked, 'Ten bob, half-a-crown, shillings . . . hiv ye jist got oot o' jile, son?'"

TIME flies ... a reader points out that anyone who did National Service in Britain will be at least seventy years old this year. We remember one chap telling us he sat his motorbike test at Catterick Camp while doing his National Service. He reported to a sergeant who sent him on the motorbike to the shop for two ounces of Golden Virginia tobacco. Noting his safe return, the sarge threw two dustbin lids on the ground and told him to ride a figure of eight around them. When he managed that, he was told he had passed.

AN OBSERVATION for those who remember old Glasgow biscuit companies. Rangers' ageing defender Davie Weir struggling in Sunday's Old Firm game reminds Gary Johnston: "When another Rangers centre-half, Colin Jackson, became, according to some, a tad beyond his sell-by date, he became known as the Caramel Wafer on account of the fact that he was Grey and Done."

OUR TALES of former Glasgow football club Third Lanark remind John Bannerman of when he was a linesman there in the sixties at a reserve match and was expecting to be paid his £2.50 fee in cash.

Says John: "We went to the treasurer's office only to be told that the attendance was insufficient to cover our fees. A committee member came up with a solution: empty the one-armed bandits, and we came away loaded down with sixpences."

THIRD LANARK, continued. Martin Milarky regales us: "As a ball boy at Cathkin, I witnessed many strange incidents. After the match, players, club officials and ball boys, amazingly, gathered in the lounge to partake of sausage rolls, but it was also where the Hi-Hi players were paid. Even as an eleven-year-old, I knew it was wrong to see the great Thirds and later Celtic goalie Evan Williams paid his £8 wage by having sixty-four half-crowns from the gate money counted out while he juggled a sandwich and a cup of tea. Meanwhile, friends and cronies of chairman Bill Hiddleston knocked back the champagne feet away."

THE NAAFI, which supplies food and drink to the armed forces, celebrates ninety years of its existence. A book just published on the NAAFI's history relates that after the Falklands War there were still many British troops on the islands who liked buying souvenirs in the NAAFI shop. A best seller was a soft toy penguin – which was made in Britain, shipped 8,000 miles to the Falklands, and then taken back to Britain by the delighted troops.

NOSTALGIA alert: Bill Thomson in Bothwell recalls when folk had to send telegrams to wish relatives abroad a Good New Year. An old uncle in Dumfries some years ago sent such a message to his sister in Canada, which ended with the traditional New Year greeting "Lang May Your Lum Reek".

She still has it framed on her wall, as along the way it was typed up and sent as "Lang May Your Bum Reek".

OUR STORY about the typo in the telegram reminds Maureen Puricelli in Carluke of when her brother some years ago was a student in Spain. A fellow Scottish student, anxiously awaiting the news that he had become an uncle, finally received the telegram informing him: "It's a box!"

WE ASKED for your stories about Robert Burns, who died of course of rheumatic fever. As George Morton recounts: "Some years ago my young niece concluded her school essay on Burns with the statement that he died at the age of thirty-six, of romantic fever.

"She'd done her research, then."

BUS TALES continued. David Scott reports: "I remember travelling up Maryhill Road on my way to Firhill on the top deck of a Corporation bus in the early 1970s. It was winter and as usual all the windows were steamed up.

"There were two women behind me speaking in hushed tones until one of them screeched, 'Whit's she marryin' him fur? He hisnae goat a telly.'"

OUR NATIONAL Service stories reminded Ian Deuchar in Milngavie: "When square-bashing at RAF Wilmslow, we had a corporal drill instructor who would stick his face six inches from yours and scream at the pitch of his voice, 'I'll put my boot so far up your backside (the corporal used another word) you'll wonder why your teeth have turned black.'"

AND EDINBURGH Tory councillor Alastair Paisley reported to RAF Bridgnorth in Shropshire for his National Service basic training. "I still remember square bashing," says Alastair, "and the drill corporal shouting that if you made an error, he would pull off your arm and beat you to death with the soggy end."

TALES of Army catering remind a Kelvinside reader of lining up for food in the mess where the cooked food looked so vile he put only a piece of cake on his tray. The cook asked him if that was all he was having, and when he replied that the rest didn't look very appetising, the cook asked in that case if he would like two slices of cake.

When our reader replied in the affirmative, the cook leaned across and cut the cake on his tray in half.

OUR TALE of army cooking reminds Alun Hotchkiss: "An ex-army pal told me about the time he complained to the cook that the meat in the rabbit stew he was serving didn't look or taste like rabbit. The cook admitted that he'd run short of rabbit and had padded it out with a bit of horsemeat. When pressed about how much horsemeat he'd used, he replied, 'About 50-50 – one rabbit, one horse.'"

AS OUR National Service stories march off, Stuart Paterson recalls his induction at the centre in Glasgow's Union Street. "After the medical, and interview, you filled out a form which included a question on the job you wanted during your two years in the RAF," said Stuart.

"With typical and admirable Glasgow optimism, the recruit next to me leaned over and asked, 'Hey, Jimmy, how do you spell pilot?'"

THE ANNIVERSARY of decimalisation reminds Bill Copeland of the American sailor, on leave from the Polaris submarine base at the Holy Loch, travelling to Glasgow to try his luck at the Locarno Ballroom. The cabbie told him the fare was "seven and six" (7/6d) but the American, unfamiliar with the currency, simply held out a hand bulging with change.

The cabbie picked out half-crowns and shillings while explaining: "Seven of those and six of them."

9.
Pandamonium

The giant pandas coming to Scotland – in case you were wondering why they are on the cover – reminded a reader of the gag: "My granddad has the heart of a lion, which explains his lifetime ban from Edinburgh Zoo."

"FOLK are just copying that woman who put the cat in the wheelie bin," said the chap in the pub the other day. "I opened my bin and a wasp flew out. What sick person would have put it in there?"

LYNDA NICOLSON tells us about a Hamilton colleague whose aunt wrote a Christmas card for a new neighbour, and addressed it to Mr Candle.

She had been told his name was Mr Connell – but had assumed that was just the local pronunciation.

AFTER our story about Mr Connell being called Mr Candle by a posh woman, the great entertainer Andy Cameron contacts us: "My wee pal Hamish Colgan of Haddington was trying to impress a rather posh young lady by taking her to Edinburgh's finest restaurant.

"As they were perusing the menu a man at the next table fell to the floor and was shaking violently. Hamish tried to calm his companion by saying, 'I think he's having an epileptic foot.'"

A DOCTOR tells us that a patient complained that he couldn't hear properly. When asked if he had any previous bother, he said a number of years ago he had an operation for a perforated eardrum.

"Which ear?" asked the doc.

"Oh it must have been about 1977," replied the patient.

A CHAP in the pub claimed that he joined a gym and asked a trainer there what machine he should use to impress the ladies.

"Probably the cash machine on the wall outside," the trainer replied.

PARENTS, and even grandparents, going on Facebook, opening Twitter accounts and sending text messages, is depressing younger folk who thought it had been their sole preserve.

But not all of the oldies get it right. A West End girl tells us: "My mother thinks the abbreviation WTF stands for 'Wow that's fantastic'. So when I texted her that I had bought a new dress she merely replied 'WTF.'"

READER Ken Macdonald in Howwood wonders after a temporary hearing impairment and listening to the television news with subtitles, whether we are giving folk with hearing loss a totally different view of the world than the rest of us.

He tells us: "One example was the BBC news where a story about a maternity hospital mentioned a baby "being delivered by forceps". The subtitles stated 'as a result of being delivered by four Serbs.'"

A MOUNT FLORIDA reader on the bus into Glasgow heard a couple of chaps discussing whether they always finished a takeaway curry when they had it delivered. One of them opined: "The biggest lie I tell myself is that I'm going to eat the rest of it for lunch the next day, not over my sink at midnight the same night."

COMMONWEALTH Games news, and Bill McKelvie reads in a Scottish newspaper that Lord Coe handed over "the host city fag" to Glasgow council leader Gordon Matheson.

Considering Glasgow's health record, Bill's not convinced it was a misprint.

WE MENTIONED restaurateur Charan Gill doing stand-up shows at his Slumdog restaurant during Glasgow Comedy Festival. Naturally it reminded a few readers of the Indian waiter asking a diner: "Curry ok sir?"

"Naw, ah cannae sing a note!" he said.

And Ian Ross tells us: "Phoned the Ashoka and asked, 'Do you deliver?' They said, 'No – just chicken, lamb or beef.'"

KEITH CHAMPAN in Knightswood tells us about the young lad phoning the Ashoka and asking if they did takeaway.

When they said yes, he replied: "What's 140 minus 88?"

MATT VALLANCE recalls that when the great batsman Sachin Tendulkar was playing for Yorkshire, a Bradford curry house offered two special curries: the Boycott and the Tendulkar. "Both," says Matt, "gave you the runs, but you got them faster if you had the Tendulkar."

JOHN QUINN in Lenzie tells us of a relative with the job of delivery driver for an Indian takeaway, who got fed up with the complaints. It came to a head when a customer complained that his crispy poppadoms were broken when they arrived.

John's relative merely replied: "Whit ye greetin' aboot? Ye cannae get a whole wan in yer mooth anyhow."

"WHAT'S the difference between peaches and nectarines?" a reader phones to ask. When we fail to answer, he says: "Nectarines don't try to trade on their dad's name to get a TV series."

A CHAP in Edinburgh's Queen Street was staring at the Scottish National Portrait Gallery where scaffolding was being dismantled after some stone-cleaning. Looking at the historical figures he declared: "Honestly! You'd think they'd have repaired everything while they had the scaffolding up – that statue's missing an arm."

The woman with him squinted up and told him: "That's Nelson."

OUR BITING dogs tale reminds Allan Cook in Helensburgh of his family pet Buster, who took a dislike to the vet. Says Allan: "Our vet had a leg shot off in the last unpleasantness. Buster was smart enough to always bite the vet's good leg."

A READER who smokes – yes, there are still a few of them – has his own little joke when he buys a disposable lighter in a newsagent's. When the chap serving inevitably flicks the lighter to check it's working, our smoker tells him: "It's all right – I've been smoking for thirty years so I know how a lighter works. You don't have to show me."

AN ABERDEEN reader phones: "I bumped into a man sobbing outside a department store who told me he hates this time of year, having to dress up in a ridiculous red outfit and embarrassing himself in front of thousands of people. I told him, 'Look, Mr Hartley, it was your decision to sign for Aberdeen.'"

"I DON'T think my girlfriend is the brightest," said the chap in the pub.

"When I told her that they sometimes perform cavity searches at airports looking for drugs, she said surely you couldn't hide much drugs in your mouth."

OUR MENTION of ovens reminds Joe Hunter in Norway of his dad having the unfortunate experience of having two teeth fall out of his top set of wallies.

Says Joe: "He was resigned to going to the dentist for a new set when a workmate said that Araldite would fix it, so he bought some and fixed both teeth perfectly back into the top set.

"He then had a look at the instructions which said it would benefit from heat to make the glue fix quicker. So he popped them in the oven, checked back later, and found all his teeth floating in a pool of melted wax."

IT'S THE traditional time of year when folk vow to exercise more. A Glasgow reader hears a perky chap in his office say to a colleague: "Are you going to hit the gym after work?"

"Only if my car skids on the way to the pub," his colleague replied.

AGED relatives continued. Gerry McCulloch tells us he suggested to his mother that she should write on the back of holiday photographs when and where they were taken.

Sometime later when he was looking at them he noticed she had written: "Arran. Last week."

THE POOR health of Glaswegians reminds Jayne Burnett of attending a public health conference when a speaker announced that a man was likely to live five years longer in Edinburgh than in Glasgow.

A GP in the audience piped up: "Aye, but who would want to?"

NEW YEAR is a time for reflection. A reader tells us of her friend bemoaning the fact she was getting old by explaining: "My knees used to crack only when I crouched or knelt down very fast.

"Now when I run down stairs, it sounds like I'm microwaving popcorn."

A READER who was playing the piano at a senior citizens club in Glasgow tells us one of the ladies told him she talked herself out of a speeding ticket by telling the police officer who stopped her the reason she was going so fast is that she had to get there before she forgot where she was going.

OUR mention of the now-closed Glasgow Zoo provoked a flurry of emails from readers telling us: "Glasgow Zoo finally closed after its entire animal complement was reduced to one small dog.

"It was a Shih Tzu."

"I DROPPED my mobile phone in the bath, and wasn't sure if it would still work," said the chap in the pub.

"The wife asked if I had tried ringing it. I told her I had, but not much water came out."

"I ALWAYS like to strike a happy medium," a reader phones to tells us, "which is why I'm now banned from the British Paranormal Society's awards night."

"I WAS flicking through the magazine in my dentist's waiting room," said the chap in the pub. "Isn't it a shame what happened to Grace Kelly?"

A GLASGOW reader fears his mate might not be that bright as the two of them, plus a third friend, went on a weekend fishing expedition which involved great food, nice accommodation and a few pints, even although they only caught one fish amongst them.

Totting up the cost of the trip on the way home, our reader surmised: "That one fish cost us £450."

"What!" replied his mate. "It's a good thing we didn't catch any more."

NEIL ARTHUR on Arran tells us that for many years bagpipe tunes were named after battles, or regiments' farewells to trouble spots, such as "The Barren Rocks of Aden".

Perhaps a piper's life isn't so exciting any more, as he noted from the World Pipe Band Championships that Lothian & Borders Police band's medley included "The Day the Co-op Flooded".

A MILNGAVIE reader was phoning her friend but the phone in the kitchen was answered by her teenage son who said: "I think she's in the shower – hang on and I'll check."

Our reader thought she would then hear the phone being put down and the sound of him going upstairs. Instead, he turned the kitchen tap on, her friend howled down from upstairs that the shower was scalding, and the lad said: "Yes, she is."

READER Gordon Neish likes the can-do attitude of Google maps. If you type in seeking directions from China to Japan, it gives detailed instructions to get to Shanghai on the coast then adds: "Jet-ski across the Pacific Ocean for 782 kilometres."

OUR TALES of how confusing Scottish idioms can be to visitors reminds Andrew Murray in Greenock of how a positive can often mean a negative.

His favourite is a wee boy asking his mother for sweeties and receiving the confusing reply: "Sweeties? Ah'll gie ye sweeties!"

PROVING that Edinburgh folk really are friendly, Denise Percival tells us a colleague arrived at an Edinburgh law firm and asked the receptionist where the gents' toilet was.

"I'll just come and point you in the right direction," she replied.

"No need to go that far," replied the anxious colleague.

TRAVEL search site Skyscanner has listed the top five fish and chip shops in the world as: Publicis Drugstore Brasserie in Paris, A Salt and Battery in New York, the Frying Scotsman in Taipei, the Crispy Cod in Fuengirola, and Atlantic Fast Food in Coatbridge. We only mention it as a reader once claimed you could never mention Paris, New York and Coatbridge in the one sentence, and make any sense.

THE ROYAL Society for the Protection of Birds is campaigning against government cuts to countryside funding, arguing they will harm wildlife. For some reason, it reminds us of the comedian who once declared: "I bought a self-assembly bird table.

"It's been out in the garden for a month now and the chirpy wee beggars still haven't put it up."

MANY a text messenger adds LOL to their text message to indicate "laugh out loud" at an amusing incident. A reader hears a young woman on the bus tell her pal: "I find it hard to believe you laugh out loud as much as you claim to."

THE PERENNIAL question of sex among senior citizens came up at a golf club, where a chap conceded he had sex with his wife about

once a month. Others concurred, but one bold pensioner said: "With me, it's almost every night of the week."

As his mates looked awestruck, he added: "Monday, almost. Tuesday, almost. Wednesday . . ."

OCCASIONALLY we discuss misheard song lyrics. "In 'Somewhere Over the Rainbow' from *The Wizard of Oz*," asks reader John McGowan, "what was Dorothy doing 'wi' a pie'?"

GORDON MARTIN writes: "Your recent stories on misheard lyrics reminded me that my uncle was convinced that Bill Hailey was singing 'Shake Marilyn Monroe' in his classic hit.

"I guess the sound quality on 78s wasn't that great."

MISHEARD lyrics continued. Frazer Beggs in Australia says: "In the eighties my grandfather used to hear the words 'wake me up before yer cocoa' from the well known Wham! song."

ALISTAIR FULTON in Govan says: "When I was in my early twenties, I was sure I heard the Beatles singing, 'We all live in a yellow soup tureen.'

"Now I consider myself lucky to hear any words at all."

10.
Street-Life

Sometimes you witness the daftest of things, or hear the oddest of conversations out in the street. Fortunately our readers let us know.

A READER in Partick watched as two young chaps lifted up a sofa that had been left out on the pavement for refuse collection outside a block of flats. He assumed they were going to take it away for their own gaff.

But instead they turned it upside down and shook it. Two or three coins dropped on to the pavement, and the chaps put the sofa back down, collected the coins and walked on.

EVEN when celebrating a birthday, Glaswegians can't pass up the chance of a sly wee dig. A Burnside reader on an 18 bus going through the city's East End spotted a giant poster strung across a wall which declared: "Dougie Robb is fifty today. He cannae believe it."

Underneath was written: "Neither can we. We thought he was sixty."

WHAT'S happening in Glasgow these days, an ex-pat asks. Well, we pass on from Alex Robertson: "I was at the People's Palace on Sunday where a drunken Glaswegian incoherently argued with a door preserved from Duke Street Prison. He shouted aggressively while swaying back and forth, before punching said door. A small crowd of tourists gathered, presumably in the mistaken belief this was all part of the show."

A READER on the bus from Balfron into Glasgow heard a young woman from the village describing a weekend party to her pal, and announcing: "I didn't realise how drunk I was until I went to wipe something off my cheek – and realised it was the floor."

DURING Glasgow's West End Festival, a colleague of STV presenter John MacKay overheard a woman giving her other half a telling off. "We're here for the weans," she said, "no for you to get mad wi' it."

THE SUN just occasionally shining during the summer reminded Hugh Nicolson of walking through Govan when a grimfaced local lady in her fifties, wearing a three-quarter-length coat, came out with one of those memorable Glasgow comments.

She told her two diminutive pals as they passed Hugh: "I don't care whit embday says, this coat's cummin' aff."

JOHN LAWSON from West Kilbride was passing the cement works just south of Dunbar on the A1 when he noticed a large road sign

reading "Cement Works". Underneath, someone had added: "If you get the mix right."

ONLY in the West End one suspects . . . Rony Bridges was standing on Byres Road reading a *Big Issue* he had bought when a woman took it out of his hands and gave him £2. He feels he was perhaps just a tad too casually dressed. Or as a friend cruelly remarked on his dress sense: "You been running through Oxfam again with sticky tape on?"

A PUB discussion in Edinburgh was about the news that iPhones have a built-in tracking device which monitors everywhere the owner goes. Although some in the discussion expressed their anger at such a thing, one sage pointed out: "What's the big deal? It's not as if iPhone users don't tell you on Facebook where they are every five minutes anyway."

A READER who was having a fag outside a Byres Road pub was approached by a mendicant who asked: "Excuse me pal, any chance of a fag?"

Our reader not unreasonably pointed out: "You're already smoking one, mate."

"Just planning for the future," the beggar replied.

WE LIKE to hear about visitors to Glasgow and what they see. John Stewart in Saltcoats recounts: "On a visit to the Glasgow Science Centre with our grandson we were, as always, fascinated by the incredible technology and engineering on display. However, as we were leaving the car park our parking token failed to raise the barrier. On pressing the emergency button provided I was promptly told to 'gie the machine a clatter, pal'. Of course this worked – true Glasgow technology!"

THE BIGGEST growth area in recent years has been social network sites such as Facebook where folk describe themselves in glowing terms. One student we spotted in the West End yesterday was wearing a T-shirt with the heartfelt message across the front: "I wish I were more like my online persona."

SOME overheard conversations stick in the mind. Neil Mackenzie from Cunninghamhead in Ayrshire was in an Italian restaurant in Kilmarnock last week when he heard a diner ask her companion: "What's veal?"

"I think it's deer," he hazarded a guess.

"No it's not," she replied. "It's cheaper than steak."

ONLY in Glasgow . . . Judy Thomson was watching BBC Reporting Scotland on the arrest in Glasgow connected with the Stockholm terrorist bombing. A neighbour was interviewed about the armed police raid, and said: "I heard a lot of noise which woke me up. Police were shouting, 'Lie down, lie down.' Doors were banging, there were firearms."

The neighbour added: "I thought it must be the end of a party or something."

UNUSUAL dog names attracted our attention recently. Gaynor Allan, who runs the Ruff Rovers dog-walking service in Milngavie, tells us she bumped into a chap with a Staffordshire bull terrier that he called Giro.

Says Gaynor: "I thought it was because he ran around in circles, until the owner said, 'It's what unemployed people get.'"

LINGUISTIC mix-ups remind Robert Calder of his brother working on a film shoot in Glasgow on a really cold day when the English director asked one of the Glasgow kids involved if he was cold. "I'm freezin'!" the youngster replied.

"How about you?" the director asked the next lad.

"Am urny," he replied.

"Lovely to meet you Ernie," responded the director.

A SENIOR citizen in Motherwell tells us he was just about to go into a town centre newsagent's to buy a lottery ticket when he slipped on the ice and dropped the pound coin he had in his hand.

A young chap behind him politely said: "I'll get that for you, sir."

Our reader was pondering on the politeness of today's youth when the chap picked up the coin and did a runner.

A LONDON visitor to Glasgow tells us she is always impressed by west of Scotland parenting skills. But we think she was joking.

When we asked for an example, she told us: "I was in Buchanan Street on Saturday when a child was screeching to his mother over and over that he wanted to go to McDonald's.

"Eventually, in sheer exasperation, she tugged him along and shouted: 'It'll be Smackdonald's you'll get if ye don't shut up.'"

YES, IT'S a stressful time in the shops before Christmas, and a reader in Buchanan Street heard a woman lecture an older woman: "What's the point in having a smoke detector if you never put a battery in it?"

And the older woman snapped back: "What's the point in having a daughter if all she does is ask stupid questions?"

MOST Scots have been commenting on how cold it was last winter. A Dennistoun reader was much taken with the woman in his local shop who declared: "It was that cold my da's teeth were chatterin' – and they were still in the glass!"

IT CAN be confusing for some, it seems, working out which mendicants on the streets of Glasgow are homeless. Steven McKenzie was at Glasgow's Central Station when a chap approached a commuter and asked with hand extended: "I need to pay my electricity. Can you help?"

The sceptical commuter replied: "That's some kitted-out box you stay in, mate."

OUR STORY about billboards reminded Brian Ross of the giant one near Glasgow's Queen Street Station some years ago that had a health poster about rising levels of sexually transmitted diseases, and giving the number of the clinic to call.

Next to it was a poster of a cheery Glesga wifie carrying a shopping basket with the caption: "I got it at the Co-op."

A MOTHER was seen arguing with her young daughter on Glasgow's Byres Road when she suddenly snapped at the girl: "I should have called you Google – you've got an answer for everything."

A PARTICK reader was amongst the large crowd on Dumbarton Road held back because of the police siege on the flat where a chap had barricaded himself in.

She tells us: "Two old dears pushed to the front and asked what was going on. 'The polis are watching that,' a chap replied. 'The guy's keepin' a hostage up there.'

"'Hear that, Mary?' said the woman to her pal. 'The police are here with their guns 'cause somebody's keeping horses in his flat.'"

11.
On The Road

Travel may or may not broaden the mind, but it can give you a laugh.

AN ENGLISH chap working in Glasgow was telling his colleagues in the pub: "I got a train to Airdrie the other night. The ticket chap said it would be 19:45 when we arrived.

"He was being a bit harsh – it looked more like the early sixties to me."

MHAIRI PEARSON was on the 44 bus in Glasgow when she heard a teenage girl tell her mum: "I wish I had bigger boobs." Her mother gave the advice: "Eat doughnuts. It worked for me."

A DRIVING test examiner swears he asked a woman learner to reverse around a corner. Unfortunately, the car came to a halt at least three feet from the pavement.

"Could you get a little closer?" he asked her.

She unbuckled her seatbelt, slid over towards him, and asked: "Now what?"

MATT DUFFY tells us that when he was driving a cab at Anniesland in Glasgow, a little old lady passenger accused taxi drivers of sticking their bottles of Irn-Bru beside the meter as the iron in the drink made the meters go round faster.

"Youse are aw robbers, so ye ur," she added.

A PSYCHIATRIST tells us: "Denial, anger, bargaining, depression, then acceptance."

She added: "The five stages to buying petrol."

A READER recalls the late great polymath and football pundit Bob Crampsey who explained at a dinner that on the way, his taxi driver asked: "Are you thon Bob Crampsey that won the Brain of Britain on the radio?"

On proudly confirming that he was indeed, he was somewhat deflated with the reply: "Do you no' get hacked off being mistaken for that clown that does the fitba?"

EDINBURGH tram boss David Mackay resigned, describing the project as "hell on wheels". A reader says: "If he thinks that's hell on wheels, then he's obviously never been on a Glasgow late-night bus on a Friday."

A READER overhears an old chauvinist at his golf club pontificate: "Did you see that bad drivers are to be hit with £100 fixed penalty fines?

"No doubt the feminists will soon be telling us it's a sexist law."

GLASGOW'S Queen Street Station is of course a terminus. That would seem obvious from the row of buffers facing the trains. Nevertheless, Dave Martin in Dundee tells us he was catching the Glasgow to Dundee train at Queen Street when a group of American tourists came on.

One of them asked the Scottish chap across the table from him if he knew if his seat was forward facing.

"I hope not," replied the Scot. "Otherwise we'd be heading for George Square."

A FRUSTRATED Dunblane reader who spends much of his time travelling on business asks: "Did you know that the smallest unit of speed is the Stobart?"

He explains: "It is the difference in speed between a lorry overtaking on a dual carriageway, and the speed of the lorry it is overtaking."

A CHAP in the pub at the weekend, where the discussion was on the rising cost of living, declared: "I was at the garage where the petrol came to £39.99, so I give the pump a little squeeze to round it up.

"Went in to pay and the cashier said, 'That'll be £44.78.'"

MOTORWAY signs continued. Says John Cochrane, "The overheard sign said: 'Breakdown Junction 22'. When I got there I just burst into tears."

THE PRICE of fuel continues to vex folk it seems. A reader in a West Lothian village spotted a van parked in the street with a sign propped on the dashboard stating: "No petrol kept in this van overnight."

A READER on the 9 bus in Glasgow heard an old dear tell her friend that the husband of a mutual friend had just died.

"Was it cancer?" the pal asked.

"No, nothing that serious," replied the pensioner.

"WHEN I bought my car," said the chap in the pub at the weekend, "the salesmen said it would last a lifetime."

He added: "I didn't realise he was referring to the payments."

MUNGO HENNING in Ayrshire thought the tyres on his wife's car looked a bit soft so drove it to the garage to check. When he asked the attendant for a 20p piece for the air compressor he was told it now took a 50p piece. When he queried such a large increase in price, the chap told him: "That's inflation for you."

BUS drivers have to ask the destination from holders of free bus passes, which can cause confusion.

Charles Fletcher tells us of a wee wummin on a Glasgow bus sitting down next to a friend of his and declaring: "What a lovely man yon driver is.

"He asked me where I was going and I said I was off to meet my pal for a coffee. Isn't he kind to care?"

A FORMER driving test examiner tells us about a middle-aged driver in Ayrshire sitting her test who found the road blocked by a van of workies half-heartedly unloading scaffolding. She asked the examiner what to do, and he replied, as he had to: "Do what you would normally do in such circumstances."

She then surprised him by getting out of the car and shouting at the workmen: "Wid youse idle b******* shift that truck tae ah get past, yer haudin' up ma drivin' test."

The truck was immediately shifted, but the lady failed her test.

WE ASKED for your driving test tales and Jim Scott recalls: "When I sat my first test in Shettleston, the examiner says, 'Take the next on the right,' which I did, which turned out to be the car park of a social club, so he says, 'I told you take the next street on the right!' and I argued that he didn't. I think I compounded it by asking, 'Since we are here do you fancy a pint?' Stony silence, and then he failed me.

"Next time I sat it in Carntyne to avoid him, and passed, even though it was ten to four and the weans from Smythcroft school were trying to impale themselves on my car."

A LANARK reader driving his family to visit relatives in Devon couldn't believe it when one of his youngsters asked soon into the journey the inevitable: "Are we nearly there yet?" He tried to nip this line of questioning in the bud by telling his kids that they wouldn't reach their destination until after it was dark.

His hopes of a question-free journey were dashed when his youngster asked shortly afterwards: "Is it nearly dark yet?"

MANY fathers will sympathise with Glasgow stand-up Raymond Mearns who explained that his teenage daughter thought Raymond drove a "magic taxi".

"Not only," said Raymond, "did she expect it to take her from the house to anywhere she wanted to go to in Glasgow, but at the end of the journey I had to hand her a tenner instead of the other way round."

AFTER our tale of driving instructions, Jim Cunningham tells us of a pal who had started taking driving lessons, and who was sitting behind his mum and dad in the family car, with his dad driving.

"As he was now the 'expert' on driving," says Jim, "he spent the journey constantly giving his father advice from the back seat on how his father should be negotiating the route.

"Eventually his father turned to the rear of the car and asked him, 'Look, who's driving this car? You or your mother?'"

AUTHOR Daniel Gray was travelling to Ayr for a Partick Thistle match when he got stuck at the Central Station ticket machine behind an older couple struggling to work it.

The young chap behind him rather unfairly said: "This is exactly why old people shouldn't be allowed to use technology. They two are like my maw pointing the TV remote at the kettle."

OUR TALES of buses remind a south-side reader of catching his regular No. 4 bus from Buchanan Street that goes past his road end before travelling on to Kilmarnock. One night he fell asleep and woke up in Kilmarnock, nearly thirty miles further than he wanted to go.

Seeing that the driver was a regular on the route, he said to him: "You know where I normally get off. Why didn't you wake me?"

"You looked so peaceful I didn't have the heart to," the driver replied.

THE SNOW causing travel disruption reminded Douglas Kinnaird of being at Maxwell Park Station in Glasgow on a previous inclement day when the train arrived. As the doors opened, a business chap imperiously told the ticket collector: "Perhaps you should only run trains when it snows. This is the first time this week the 8.47 has been on time."

"It's the 8.17," replied the ticket chap.

AH THE irony of the film organisation Bafta cancelling its showing in Glasgow of the latest Coen Brothers film because of the inclement weather. Name of the film? *True Grit*.

CLEARLY a fan of the west of Scotland vernacular, Stewart MacKenzie asks: "Can they not make up their minds? Signs are appearing all over the place: 'Road Closed – Snow'. Well which is it?"

A READER hears a young woman on the bus into Glasgow tell her pal that she had bought her boyfriend a special presentation box of Jack Daniel's whiskey with an engraved crystal glass for Christmas. She then added: "I told my mum I had got him a Jack Daniel's presentation box. She told me she thought he was too old for a magic set."

THE BAD weather meant people turning to alternative transport, and one Glasgow traveller, new to First buses, asked the Polish driver for a "Noddy ticket". He stared at her blankly. So she insisted: "I was told to ask for a Noddy ticket." Still no response.

At that, the chap behind her spoke up: "She wants an all day ticket."

"I TOOK the advice," said the chap in the pub, "not to travel in bad weather without a shovel, flask, wellies and a blanket."

"Mind you," he added, "I got a lot of funny looks on the bus."

A MOTHERWELL reader was impressed that a young neighbour was out washing her small Fiat car at the weekend, despite it being a cold, grey day.

After covering the car in warm soapy water, the girl extemporised by using a watering can from the garage to wash the soap off.

At that, a passing van driver wound down his window and shouted at her: "You're wasting your time – these things never grow."

GLASGOW buses continued. Rod Macfarlane recalls in his young days being a conductor on the 64 bus to Yoker when a chap came on, his eye ballooned up to the size of a melon, clutching an iron in his hand.

Says Rod: "He just stood there, then proceeded to shout out to the whole bus, 'Does anywan want tae buy an iron?'

"I asked him why he was wanting to sell it and he replied, 'Because she hit me wi' it once and she is no gonnae do it again.'"

A READER heard a motorist in his local garage mutter about £1.30 for a litre of petrol being highway robbery – then watched him pay £1.60 for a half-litre bottle of water.

LIZANNE MacKENZIE in Dumfries was visiting Glasgow when she told her taxi driver that there seemed to be an awful lot of potholes in the streets.

"Some o' thae potholes are that big," her driver replied, "I saw two Chilean miners coming out o' one o' them."

MAIRI CLARK was on the bus when an old chap came on and sat down beside a pal.

After exchanging a few tales, the chap asked his mate out of the blue: "Do you have a passport?"

His pal replied: "Not on me. I'm only going to Tesco."

A READER on the bus heard some young chaps discuss their respective girlfriends with one claiming his was not the brightest. As he explained: "She was on the bus coming to meet me, so I phoned her to find out how long she would be. When I asked her, 'Whereabouts are you?' she said she was sitting near the back."

SPOTTED on the back of a car in Bilsland Drive in Glasgow, a sticker stating, "I'm not drunk – just avoiding the potholes."

DONALD GRANT in Paisley heard two senior citizens extolling the benefits of their free bus passes, with one of them declaring it was good exercise. When his pal asked how the bus pass helped with fitness, his mate replied: "Ah jump oan and aff the buses in the morning 'til ah find a free copy of the Metro."

ANNE BENYON tells us she was listening to presenter Steve McKenna on Real Radio who explained he was trying to phone someone who had requested a song, but couldn't get through to him. After playing the song, McKenna announced: "I just got a text from him saying he would like to pick up the phone, but cannae 'cos he's on a bus with a group of neds."

A STIRLING reader travelling by train to Edinburgh on Friday had to endure standing room only in the crowded carriage while the conductor apologised, stating: "This is due to the school holidays and the Edinburgh Festival."

"Which of these," wondered our passenger to himself, "took ScotRail by surprise?"

AND A Newton Mearns reader on the train into Glasgow watched as a retired gentleman searched his pockets for his ticket when asked for it by the guard. Seeing how frantic the chap was, the ScotRail chap told him: "It's OK. I'm sure you've got one."

"I still need to find it," the old chap replied. "I've forgotten where I'm going."

A READER buying his car insurance on a popular online site noted a message popped up asking: "Would you also like a quote to insure your pet?"

He thought to himself: "Surely no-one lets their dog drive the car."

CLARE HENDRY tells us she was on a 44 bus in Glasgow when fellow passengers became concerned about a chap slumped in his seat, either drunk or asleep. The driver told them the chap had been on the bus for more than two hours. At this, one concerned customer argued: "You must have been to the terminus and back, and you didn't say anything?"

At that, a fellow passenger came to the driver's defence and said: "Perhaps the boy's goat an all-day ticket."

12.
Boats And Planes

THE SCENE: Glasgow Airport. The weather: stormy.

Guy Wadge, from Helensburgh was preparing to fly with a colleague to Amsterdam.

"It was so windy that the plane was being blown around quite a lot before it had even taken off. We were already delayed because of the weather and there were rumours that the flight would be cancelled, but we finally got the go-ahead.

"My colleague, unfortunately, suffers from piles, and he started to blow up a cushion to sit on.

"Cue the Glaswegian voice behind us: 'Hell's teeth, they're blowing up the life jackets already!'"

THE PADDLE steamer *Waverley* had a hectic summer on the Clyde. A reader on board tells us about a young mother who disembarked at Dunoon and, while watching the ship chug away, suddenly became slightly agitated and shouted to her sister on board: "Watch ma wean! Ah forgot it!"

The wean was indeed still on aboard asleep in its buggy. Fortunately mother and child were reunited later.

SHAUN MURPHY in Kilbirnie passes on: "My daughter, who works for an airline, told me that one of her colleagues was explaining to first-class passengers where the emergency exits were on the upper deck of the aircraft, and that in the unlikely event of a landing on water, they would have to escape using the exits downstairs.

"A rather posh gent inquired, 'Does that mean economy gets off first?'"

CHATTY pilots, and Gilbert MacKay in Newton Mearns recounts: "I was on the Glasgow to London first flight of the day when the pilot announced, 'Lynn, our chief steward, is leaving BA today to get married.' He then added, 'Nobody even told us she was pregnant.'"

THE ASH cloud stranding passengers at Glasgow Airport reminds Sandy Ferrar, who once worked there, of reasons why you might be happy to spend your holiday at Glasgow Airport:

- Mosquitoes are not a problem.
- You'll save a fortune on sun tan lotion.
- You might be interviewed by a TV news team.
- You can manage without a phrase book – unless you're from Edinburgh.
- Airports don't crash due to volcanic dust.

WE MENTIONED the punning names of horses that owners try to sneak past the horse racing authorities. Boat owners also like their puns it seems. A reader tells us one boat he saw on the Thames was called *Sir Osis of the River*. And another reader asked a boat owner why he had called his craft *After You*.

"So that I can tell women I'm chatting up," he replied, "that I've named my boat after you."

TOM NUGENT in Troon tells us: "I observed *Maiden Taiwan* at Millport, which looked as if it had been constructed in a local garage."

YACHT names continued. Brendan Docherty at Cairnbaan on the Crinan Canal tells us: "I see an interesting array of leisure craft pass my window. One in particular stands out – a large and very expensive cabin cruiser crewed by a happy crowd of gin-drinking fifty-somethings. The boat's name – *Sorry Kids*."

IAIN MANN says he was on an early morning flight from Glasgow to Heathrow when the captain came on the intercom and said they would soon be landing at Jersey where the weather was glorious sunshine. After a few minutes of animated discussion among the bleary-eyed passengers wondering whether they had got on the wrong plane, the captain came back on to apologise and to remind them it was April 1. At that a passenger sent a stewardess forward with a message for the captain stating that if it was alright with him, the passengers would still prefer to go to Jersey.

CHATTY pilots continued. Ian Barnett had flown with friends from Glasgow to Campbeltown to play at Macrihanish Golf Club on a blustery day. Says Ian: "After a bumpy approach, we finally got down, and the pilot turned round and said, 'You might have thought that was a difficult landing – but not half as difficult as it will be for you lot to tee off at the first.'"

CHATTY pilots continued. Bill Cassidy tells us: "I was on a red-eye shuttle to London, when the pilot piped up, 'Good morning ladies and gentlemen, I hope none of you is a first-time or nervous flier, as this is also my first flight.'

"After a short pause he added, 'Today!'

"Oh how we laughed."

PETER NIVEN in Western Australia knew he was back home in Scotland when, on a recent trip, his wife spotted a basket with a small selection of fruit in the cafeteria on the Rothesay ferry and selected a pear.

Approaching the counter, she asked the attendant: "How much for the pear?"

"Dunno," came the reply, "No-one's bought fruit before."

"Ach, just keep it."

A READER waiting for his flight at Glasgow Airport watched as a chap ran up to the next gate, just making his flight in the nick of time.

The flight attendant taking his boarding pass asked: "Rushing?" Our reader doesn't know if the out-of-breath passenger was joking when he replied: "No, Scottish."

CHATTY pilots continued. John Neil recalls: "I was once on the rickety old mail plane from Stornoway to Inverness.

"It was the middle of winter, really stormy weather and it was touch-and-go if the flight would go ahead.

"After boarding, the co-pilot came out, gave us a rudimentary safety demonstration and said, 'People pay good money at Alton Towers for what you are about to experience folks. So enjoy the ride!'"

TALKING of boats, David Steele tells us about the chap who had a yacht moored at Millport named *Vengeance*, possibly in homage to the nuclear submarine that occasionally sails past.

It seems the chap, called Hamish, had taken out a loan to buy the yacht, and on the day the final payment was made, he proudly wore a T-shirt around town with the slogan: "Vengeance is mine!"

BOAT names continued. A reader tells us that the protocol when using VHS radio to contact a boat is to repeat its name three times. He reckons the boat owner on the west coast who named his vessel *Woof* knew this, as it causes much hilarity to hear the Coastguard contacting the boat and going "*Woof, Woof, Woof*".

"THERE used to be a boatyard at the Broomielaw," says Jack Docherty, "which had a boat with the name *Sloop du Jour*."

BOAT names continued. Robert Armstrong in Houston says: "At the marina on the Toronto Islands, I was amused by the honesty of one yacht owner who had named his craft *Raison Debt*. I also recall an owner at Ullapool who named his craft *How Much?* as that was his wife's response on hearing of its purchase."

BOAT names continued. *Morning Mist* is of course a favourite boat name. Jack Bisset, however, wonders how much the owner of a boat on Loch Lomond enjoyed going to the pub of an evening as he had named his craft *Morning Missed*.

WE FINALLY weigh anchor on boat names with:

Bobby Holden spotted on the Crinan Canal – *Maid Freya Kitt*.

Gordon Sutherland was at Kingsridge School in Drumchapel when pupils built a yacht and had to choose a name that connected it to Kingsridge. Alas *Sin King* was rejected.

A Helensburgh reader saw in the Gareloch, *Mama's Mink*.

AEROPLANE seating continued. Jennifer Wilkie tells us she was waiting in the departure lounge of Boston Airport for a flight to Glasgow when her husband, being annoying, told her to go up to the desk and try to get an upgrade.

Shaking her head, she went up to the desk, and said sarcastically, as many Scottish women do: "His lordship was wondering about an upgrade."

She didn't expect the woman behind the desk to squeal: "Oh my gawd, his lordship!" and promptly change their seats to first class.

"DID YOU see that American airline Southwest grounded its older Boeing 737s when a 5ft hole appeared in one plane's fuselage?" said the chap in the pub.

"If it was Ryanair," said his pal, "they would probably just charge you extra for having a sunroof."

A BEARSDEN reader tells us he was catching an easyJet flight to London and was mildly surprised when an attractive woman boarded the half-full plane, and decided to sit next to him.

After chatting for a while his ego was deflated when she told him: "I was nervous as this is my first flight on my own. My mum said sit next to someone who looks trustworthy, and you look just like my dad."

OUR MENTION of cabin crew reminds a Glasgow business traveller: "British Airways' more sniffy stewards have devised a collective name for the poor folk lumped together back in the World Traveller cabin, which is the airline's name for economy. It's World Chav-eller, to reflect their distaste at the riff-raff they now have to look after."

13.
Politics

Politics, say some people, is no laughing matter. But fortunately Diary readers disagree.

A BIG political story was the Scottish Tory manifesto stating that children should be able to leave school at fourteen to learn a trade.

"Or as one chimney sweep told me," phoned a reader, "back to the good old days."

POLITICS, and Clark McGinn tells us: "I was in a Dublin taxi as the dust was settling after their election. I asked the driver for his opinion on the change of government. He replied, 'New circus – same clowns.'"

DO POLITICIANS have a sense of humour? First Minister Alex Salmond was asked to contribute to the book *Why Am I Laughing?*, a collection of jokes to raise money for a Scottish dementia charity. Says Alex: "What do you call a man who is nearly home?

"Hamish." Well it made us laugh.

READERS who occasionally have to make speeches in public will feel sympathy for Bailie Phil Greene of Glasgow City Council who revealed, at the opening reception of the Glasgow International Comedy Festival, that his wife was not with him. He explained: "She said to me, 'You'll tell a joke, it will fall flat, and I'll be embarrassed. So I'm not going.'"

But actually Phil did make us laugh in an ironic way. He apologised for being late as the Lord Provost's limo was sent to collect him – and it got a flat tyre thumping into one of the potholes on the road that the council is supposed to maintain.

A SCOT serving in southern Afghanistan tells us about a Nato official who was keen to hear from ordinary Afghans how their lives had improved since the Taliban had been pushed out.

He asked a carpenter in the bazaar if business was good and was surprised when the chap said no.

"Oh," replied the Nato official, "I thought it would have been great. We've been knocking down lots of doors recently."

THE ARAB SPRING, and after the Egyptian Army issued a statement saying they would not resort to the use of force, an old army type tells us: "So the same tactics they used in the Six-Day War against Israel?"

AND OF course we are inundated with the West of Scotland text message which states: "The Egyptian Government wants the protesters to chill out by getting in their cars and sounding their horns.

"They're calling it the Toot 'n' Kalm Doon."

THE INTERNATIONAL war on terror, and a Newton Mearns reader reports: "On Sunday while having lunch with my family, I noticed that my granddaughter was very quiet. After a bit I asked what was wrong with her. She replied that she was upset because someone had shot Aladdin."

MANY Irish were celebrating St Paddy's Day in Glasgow while putting Ireland's economic woes out of their minds. Apart from one student type who wore a T-shirt with a sad leprechaun on it. Below it read: "Ireland. Turns out the pot of gold was empty."

DENIS MacCANN, outgoing manager of Glasgow's Holiday Inn, told guests at the Holiday Inn's St Patrick's Day breakfast that Ireland was the first country to set up a "global social network".

"Or, as other countries call it," said Denis, "emigration."

A KEEN observer of European politics, watching the Eurovision Song Contest, explains how the votes were cast: "So it's eight points to the country to the left of you, ten points to the country to the right of you, and twelve points to the country that bailed you out."

And another opined: "So the rest of Europe likes us enough to sing in our language, but not enough to vote for us?"

NATURALLY Osama bin Laden's death has been the talk of the steamie.

As one chap in the pub opined: "I don't blame him for having phone numbers secretly sewn into his clothes. My wife found a phone number in my pocket once and there was all hell to pay."

SO ARE Diary readers feeling sorry for the Lib Dems after their shocking Scottish elections result? Em, not really. A political activist swears that on the notice board at the Scottish Parliament is a card reading: "For sale, sixteen-seater minibus, surplus to requirements. Would swap for nice five-seater car.

"Phone Tavish on . . ."

AND ANOTHER claims he went up to a Lib Dem and, putting his arm around his shoulder, told him: "Sorry you can't play in the rugby sevens this year. Will we put you down for the football five-asides instead?"

FEARS that outgoing Scottish Labour leader Iain Gray has been emasculated by his decision to give up the leadership appears to have been confirmed. The parliamentary aide to Fife Labour MSP Helen Eadie has emailed Labour Party workers at the Scottish Parliament offering them a taste of home-baked goods. Or as she stated in her email: "Sorry for those not in the Parli building, but for those who are, there is plum and frangipane tart in my office made from Iain Gray's very own plums! First-come, first-served!"

AT DUNDEE Sheriff Court, a sheriff asked for a psychiatric report on an accused who appeared a bit disturbed. It was later reported to the sheriff that no psychiatrists were available from Murray Royal Hospital as they were all required to attend a visit by First Minister Alex Salmond.

For some reason, this provoked merriment in the court.

OUR WESTMINSTER contact phones to tell us: "A lot of the damage at the London protest march has been blamed on the organisation UK Uncut.

"This is in contrast to all the damage done in Scottish cities at the weekend which is blamed on Scotland half-cut."

"CAN YOU believe," said the chap in the pub, "that Gordon Brown is being tipped to be the new boss of the International Monetary Fund?"

"That's about as likely," replied his mate, "as Tony Blair going on to be UN Peace Envoy to the Middle East.

"Oh wait."

EVEN the Government's proposed health service changes in England have an amusing side, says reader Jim Renton. He tells us the British Medical Association asked its members what they thought.

The dermatologists advised not to make any rash moves, the neurologists thought the Government had a lot of nerve, the ophthalmologists deemed the idea short-sighted, the radiologists could see right through it, the urologists were p***** off with the whole idea, and the pathologists argued: "Over my dead body!"

WELL done everyone who helped raise millions of pounds on Red Nose Day. The only person less than charitable was a Labour contact in Westminster who phoned to tell us: "Red Nose Day – the one day of the year the Liberal Democrats' Nick Clegg can hide his brown one."

SOME Glasgow chaps were discussing how dense a mate was when one declared: "He's that stupid he thinks Tripoli is a big girl's bra size."

AFTER the Budget, Martin Morrison in Lochinver says: "My wife passed her driving test last week. Domestic harmony is thus enhanced as yet one more task is shared – now neither of us can afford petrol."

THE LATEST news from Tripoli, a reader tells us, is that Abdelbaset Ali Mohmed al-Megrahi, the man convicted of the Lockerbie bombing,

is unconcerned by the bombing, riots and guns being fired. "He is telling people it's just like Greenock on a Saturday night," says our reader.

OUR POLITICAL contact in Westminster phones to tell us: "It was Lib Dem leader Nick Clegg's birthday last week. His wife had promised him a Ferrari, which never materialised. But she knew Nick could hardly lecture her on not keeping your promises."

A DISCUSSION was taking place in an Ayrshire pub about the self-assessment tax deadline having just passed, with one regular opining: "Someone here said you should pay your taxes with a smile. I tried that, but they wanted cash."

THE BUDGET reminds James Stewart in Hamilton of attending a House of Commons debate, which he later told an elderly aunt about.

Says James: "When we explained the voting division where the ayes go to the right and the noes to the left, she halted us to ask how can your nose possibly go left when your eyes go right?"

A SOUTH-SIDE reader phones to say: "If any more politicians are jailed in the UK, then we are likely to move to third in Amnesty International's list of regimes with political prisoners?"

A READER in London tells us he was at a comedy show the other night in which one of the acts told the audience: "The English are worried about the euro being introduced here because they fear the loss of national identity and prices rising.

"In Scotland, they are just worried in case it means Poundstretcher has to close."

GUEST speaker at the Trades House of Glasgow annual dinner, Tory MSP Jackson Carlaw, said he once spoke at a ladies' club lunch where he asked how long he should speak for.

The chairwoman imperiously told him: "You speak for as long as you like, Mr Carlaw, but we will be getting the bus at a quarter past two."

BELLSHILL-BORN Celtic chairman John Reid, former Cabinet minister, was commenting on Tony Blair's admission he worried about his drinking as he would have a few G&Ts and a couple of glasses of wine of an evening.

"Where I come from, they give more than that to the budgie," remarked John.

14.
Students

It's tough being a student with fewer job possibilities, and tuition fees and loans to consider. But they still make us laugh.

A STUDENT at Strathclyde Uni was telling his classmates that his dad, before the term started, told him: "You're going to be meeting a lot of girls at the university, so I got you something at the chemist's."

As the student "got a bit of a riddie" as he put it, his dad stammered: "No, I meant this deodorant."

THESE are tough times for school leavers and students looking for a job. An HR worker in a Glasgow firm wonders if it was simply nerves which made one prospective employee, on the job application form after the name of his school, when asked "Dates attended" put in "Monday, Tuesday, Wednesday, Thursday and Friday".

AS STUDENTS returned to uni after the summer break, a south-side reader heard one student on the train at Whitecraigs tell his mate: "My mum opened an official-looking letter to me which turned out to be a big fine for not returning books to the uni library."

"Was she mad?" asked the pal.

"No," replied the student. "She was just delighted that I had actually been to the library."

ST ANDREWS UNIVERSITY has many American students who occasionally suffer a bit of culture shock in Scotland. A reader in the Fife town tells us of overhearing one such student tell his pal: "I like these yellow lines to show you where the sidewalk ends."

WITH the university going back, we asked for your student tales, and Grant Melville in Falkirk tells us they once entertained themselves in

their Edinburgh student flat by tying a bottle opener on a cord, and hanging it out of the window so that it would tap mysteriously on the downstairs neighbour's window.

Finally needing the bottle-opener, hours later they hauled it back up only to find on the cord an empty beer bottle with a note inside it stating, "Cheers pal."

RUSSELL SMITH tells us about a medical student friend doing a clinical examination on the ward during his final year. The old lady in the bed was trying to help him in his diagnosis, and quietly told him: "I know I'm not supposed to tell you this but I heard two doctors saying I don't have two neurones to rub together."

A NORTH KELVINSIDE reader having a pint in Byres Road heard a student tell his pal: "I'm thinking of changing my name to Domhnall."

"Is that Gaelic?" asked his mate. "What does it mean?"

"It's Gaelic for 'hoping this will fool the Student Loans Company'," the chap replied.

A HYNDLAND reader on the train into town saw a little girl point at Glasgow University and ask her dad what that place was.

He replied: "It's a school for big people," before adding, "big people who don't want to work."

WE DIDN'T realise how tough it was for students these days until Jamie Kelly in Kilmacolm told us about his aunt who volunteers in a

Stirlingshire charity shop where a student came in and said he needed a smart outfit as he had got a part-time job as a barman. After finding a white shirt, black trousers, belt and tie for him, she took pity on him as he was so desperate for shoes he said he would take any size between five and twelve, so she only charged him £2.50 for the outfit.

The following week a uni mini-bus arrived at the charity shop crammed with students who asked for "the wee wummin wi the glasses".

OUR STORY of the student in the charity shop reminds Gary Johnston: "I spotted a cracking pair of Italian hand-made leather brogues

in a Paisley charity shop. I approached the lady behind the counter to enquire how much. '£3,' she told me in a no-nonsense fashion — and then seeing my delighted look, hastily added, 'each.'"

A STUDENT in Glasgow's West End was complaining about having no money. His pal asked him: "On a scale of one to Ireland, how broke are you?"

A READER hears a student in Glasgow's West End declare: "I didn't answer a couple of questions in my politics exam – but I think I should get extra marks for that. After all, that's what politicians do."

IN BYRES Road a student was saying that her new glasses didn't seem to be helping her eyesight much before adding: "But I cheated on the eye exam, so it's really my own fault."

When her pal asked why she had done such a stupid thing, she explained: "I'm just very competitive."

A STUDENT tells us he was in Sauchiehall Street when an ambulance was called for a girl who had been taken unwell on a night out. A lad she had met that night volunteered to go with her to the hospital but his mate pulled him aside and said: "Are you sure you want to do that? You've still got a couple of hours to pull someone else."

TWO STUDENTS are spotted, by a reader, in a Partick supermarket. He reckons they were at university as it is surely only students who go to the supermarket with their pals.

Anyway, one of them is holding a bottle of washing liquid, reading the label and declaring: "Eh? You have to be eighteen to buy this! What do they think young people would do? Drink it?"

His more sensible friend looked at the label and told him: "That's the number of washes you get from each bottle, ya eejit."

15.
Gone But Not Forgotten

TERRIBLY sad to hear of the death of actor Gerard Kelly, who was the mainstay of King's Theatre pantos in Glasgow for years. We remember in *Aladdin* when Gerard, the eponymous hero, asked the audience if he should trust the baddie, and of course the whole theatre shouted back: "No!"

Later when Aladdin was locked in the cave, the silence was broken by a lone Glasgow voice shouting: "Well, we telt ye."

THE DEATH of firebrand shop steward Jimmy Reid reminds a reader of when Jimmy appeared on the *Parkinson Show* alongside actress Lauren Bacall. He told friends Lauren had given him her business card and told him the next time he was in New York he was to look her up.

Jimmy then added: "I'm a Clydebank boy. When would I ever be passing through New York?"

MUCH-MARRIED Liz Taylor was asked at one of her later weddings by the official in charge to list her previous husbands.

"What is this? A memory test?" she replied.

Or as someone else once described her: "Always the bride, never the bridesmaid."

THE OBITUARY of Celtic player Willie O'Neill in *The Herald* – Willie was with the club in the year of the Lisbon Lions, but didn't make the European Cup-winning side – reminds a football writer of when Scottish Television, to celebrate the 25th anniversary of the Lisbon Lions, arranged a weekend for all the surviving squad members at Seamill in order to do interviews.

Researchers setting up the event couldn't trace Willie until somebody told them that he was now the janitor at St Roch's Secondary.

Says our fitba man: "Off went the invitation, Willie O'Neill duly turned up for the weekend, and it was only when Bobby Lennox asked him who he was that he replied, 'I'm Willie O'Neill, janitor at St Roch's Secondary, and I think it's great that a mere fan like me is asked along to meet my heroes.'"

It was indeed the wrong Willie O'Neill.

SAD TO hear of the death of Paisley singer/songwriter Gerry Rafferty. The story was told that session musician Raphael Ravenscroft, who played the saxophone solo on "Baker Street", was sent a cheque for £27 for the day's work – and it bounced. But Ravenscroft later recorded a Rafferty song on his own album so he couldn't have been that bothered.

Rafferty of course initially played in the Humblebums with Billy Connolly and Tom Harvey. An old colleague tells us that Connolly would introduce the band to the audience with, "We're the Humblebums," then point to Rafferty and say: "He's humble."

THE HERALD'S obituary of inspirational Montrose manager Norman Christie reminds Rod Copeland of his father playing briefly for the club. Says Rod: "He recalls that Mr Christie built a team with an emphasis on playing the ball on the ground, with good passing.

"Then one Saturday, with an upcoming cup game on the Wednesday, the chairman came to the dressing room to request that they play the ball in the air more during the game to save the pitch for the midweek match. The instructions were soon countermanded by Mr Christie."

THE DEATH of the broadcaster Robert Robinson reminded us of the time comedian Victoria Wood was pulled over by a police officer while she was driving down the motorway.

"Your tyres are very bald, madam," said the officer crossly. "You should have them replaced as soon as possible."

"Really?" said Victoria. "Couldn't I just comb the rubber over like Robert Robinson?"

THE GLASGOW Art Club in Bath Street hosted a fabulous exhibition of paintings by the late James D. Robertson, the inspirational lecturer from Glasgow Art School. The catalogue by Robin Hume includes the story: "Jimmy treasured an altercation with a lady at one of his summer schools over her use of colour. She had, she insisted,

read many books on the subject and was well acquainted with 'all the colours of the scrotum.'"

SCOTS comedian Vladimir McTavish recalled that, after the tragic death of fellow comedian Malcolm Hardee, Malcolm's brother was at his flat sorting his affairs when the phone rang. It was the Inland Revenue asking when Malcolm was going to settle his tax bill.

"When his brother informed the caller that Malcolm had died the week before, the chap said, 'Really, Mr Hardee, that's what you told us last year.'"

OUR TALE about the late comedian Malcolm Hardee's run-ins with the tax people reminds John Fleming that Malcolm, when filling in an invoice which asked for his VAT number, would simply write in his phone number and add 17.5% to the total.

THE DEATH of the great Sir Norman Wisdom reminds a reader of an EU health committee meeting in Brussels when the French chairman said they would need "la sagesse des Normands" to solve a tricky problem.

This was translated to the English speakers as: "What we need right now is Norman Wisdom."

16.
School

RETIRED modern studies teacher Colin Castle recalls teaching a fourth-year class about the Cold War and spotting one of the less diligent pupils staring out of the window.

Attracting the boy's attention, Colin asked: "I was talking about propaganda, so can you tell me what the word means?"

He stared at Colin before blurting out: "It's ma maw's real faither."

A PRIMARY teacher tells us a young charge came in without his sheet of arithmetic homework and claimed his younger brother had made it into a paper airplane.

"That's OK," replied the teacher, "we can always smooth it out."

The youngster thought again, and desperately added: "It was then hijacked."

A MOTHERWELL reader tells us his grandson came home with a new arithmetic jotter and announced that the teacher wanted it covered, and that leftover wallpaper would do.

The little one's dad piped up: "She's just a nosey-parker who wants to see what the inside of our house looks like."

A READER who grew up in Maryhill remembers struggling with his French homework. His parents, neither of whom had ever studied the language, were stumped.

As his father stared at the homework and shook his head, he mumbled: "I'm glad that I wasn't born in France – I'd never be able to speak the language."

OUR MENTION of the difficulty of learning French reminds Frank McKechnie, in Rutherglen, of the French teacher who said his son, after she had corrected some of his work, had confessed that French was like a foreign language to him.

A TEACHER on playground duty at a Glasgow Secondary heard a teenage girl shout angrily to a classmate: "Did you tell Frances ah couldnae be trusted?" She thought the reply was sheer genius.

"Naw, it wisnae me. I don't know how she found out."

TEACHERS on the Times Educational Supplement's online forum have been discussing outrageous parents. One wrote: "My sister worked in a library in Glasgow. She spotted a child using a mobile phone when they weren't so readily available, and she asked if it was her phone. She replied, 'Aye, ah've got a mobile, ma brother's got a mobile, ma mammy's got a mobile . . . an' the dug's got a pager.'

"Apparently, they'd bought a pager and attached it to the dog's collar, so that they could buzz it when it was time for it to come home and get fed."

THE FIRST day back at school reminds us of the old yarn about the little boy telling his teacher: "I don't want to alarm you, but my dad says that if my marks don't improve, someone's going to get spanked."

THE SCHOOLS are back, and so of course is the vast army of lollipop men and women. A reader in Dennistoun watched as a chap wound down the window of his car to talk to his mate who apparently had just started this week at a crossing patrol. Our reader heard the car driver shout over: "Jimmy! I always said you'd a face that could stoap traffic."

IT'S THE new school year, and an East Renfrewshire primary teacher tells us about a colleague and an assistant in the new primary one class trying to load some software onto the computer without success. When another member of staff came in to help, a wee voice from the back piped up: "You'd think they'd have someone that knew what they were doing."

A NURSERY teacher on the south side of Glasgow tells us about her new intake. A three-year-old picked up a plastic dinosaur. Holding it to her ear the child said: "Hello Mummy, when are you coming for me?"

The teacher was quite taken with this and said to the little one: "Do you want to go home?"

The tot turned to the teacher and told her: "Excuse me! I'm on the phone."

TEACHER Marion Lang tells us of a ten-year-old pupil announcing to the rest of the class, "Ma dug did a bungee jump on Saturday."

Says Marion: "His classmates were very impressed, but my scepticism cast doubt on whether dogs would really be allowed to do bungee jumps.

"The answer was, 'Naw ma dug – it was Mad Doug did the bungee jump!' The gentleman in question turned out to be a local worthy who was game for anything."

A DUNBARTONSHIRE teacher tells us she needed all these holiday weekends they get after introducing her primary class to search engines on the computer and explaining how to enter the term you want to search for, and then clicking on search.

When she asked for a suggestion, one youngster suggested typing in "mum's house keys" as his mum had been searching for hers for two days.

A LENZIE reader was not impressed by her husband when their ten-year-old son came home from school and declared that a girl in class had been yelling at him, but he didn't know what he was supposed to have done wrong.

What annoyed our reader was her husband piping up: "It's just like a lesson in being married, son."

CLASSROOMS continued. Barrie Crawford tells us: "When meeting new classes, I liked to check what pupils wanted to be called. A boy named Robert might like Rab, Bob or Bobby. Going round one class, I asked a Jennifer, 'And are you called Jennifer?'

"She stuck out her hands and replied, 'Ma hauns ur freezin' – feel them!'"

RETIRED teacher Ada McDonald recalls talking to her class about minerals, how they are found, and what they are used for.

She was then trying to turn the discussion to oil and hinted: "Factories would grind to a halt without this liquid."

A child's hand shot up and he confidently answered: "Please Miss. Tea."

GREGOR YOUNG in Castle Douglas recalls holidaying on Arran with his parents and when out one day they came across a pub, which his delighted dad described as an oasis.

It explains why the young Gregor, in school shortly afterwards, put his hand up when the teacher asked what an oasis was and emphatically replied: "A pub in the middle of nowhere."

OUR CHILDREN are under increasing pressure to do well at school these days, but one reader didn't realise how bad things were until she overheard her sons, aged six and three, getting ready the other morning.

Pressed for time, she asked the older one to help his young brother get his jacket on as he was mucking about.

She then watched him go over to his brother and announce: "Fraser. If you don't go to nursery you won't get a good job!"

CLASSROOMS continued. Should we believe Russell Smith who tells us: "I remember many years ago our second-year science class was posed the question, 'Why are there holes in a brazier?'

"Those of us who were better informed knew that the answer given by one genuine innocent, 'So that a lady wouldn't sweat too much,' was not the response that was expected.

OUR STORIES of Scots struggling to learn French remind Paul McElhone, now in Beckenham, of being so determined to pass O-Grade French, after failing previously, that he memorised an essay, "A Day in the Country". Says Paul: "When I looked at the exam paper, my heart sank. The subject was 'A Day in the Life of a Lighthouse Keeper'.

"All was not lost though. I began my essay by declaring that it was his day off and he was going to leave his island and go for a walk in the country. The first few sentences were a bit flaky, but the rest was perfect."

A BEARSDEN reader tells us he was driving his kids to school on the day before his birthday, and as usual they were fighting and squabbling in the back.

Above the din he told them: "If you behave and be kind to each other, that would be the best birthday present ever for me."

His older son replied: "Too late. I've already got you a present."

OUR SCHOOL stories remind a reader of a primary teacher telling the allscottishteachers.co.uk website of reading her P2 class a story entitled "The Speckled Hen", and asking if anyone knew what speckled meant.

One animated lad jumping up and down answered: "I know, Miss! It's got glasses!"

A READER tells us school pupils are still telling terrible jokes. His son came home from school yesterday and asked: "What's the difference between a kangaroo and a kangaroot?" He is still groaning at the answer: "One's a kangaroo, the other's a Geordie stuck in a lift."

Sorry about that.

17.
Holidays

A MILNGAVIE reader returning from holiday in Ireland liked the insouciance of his Dublin taxi driver when he urged him to step on it as he had a plane to catch.

When the driver asked when the plane was taking off, our reader replied: "An hour!" But his driver told him: "Sure we'll have time for a pint on the way."

HOLIDAYING at Easter was a Glasgow chap who had been persuaded by his family to go pony trekking in the Lake District. Being a tad dubious about the venture, he asked his wife as they were putting on their riding helmets and surveying the four-legged beasts in front of them: "How can I pick the slowest one?"

"Put a bet on it," his wife replied. "That usually works for you."

A BEARSDEN reader planning his annual Easter holiday on Lanzarote tells us he was there last year when a little boy aged about six

came running up the beach near where he was to tell his sunbathing mother in a distinctly Glasgow accent: "A big wave knocked me over and a wummin had tae help me oot."

"What was yer da doin?" asked the mum.

"Laughin," replied the wee boy.

A CHAP in a Glasgow office heard two of the younger staff discussing their summer holidays, with one girl saying she had been to Greece. When her colleague asked what it was like, the girl furrowed her brow and replied: "It's a bit like Spain – but more Greek."

JOHN THOMSON in Hamilton went on an open-top bus tour of Arran in which the driver's running commentary, desperate for interesting things to tell them, intoned: "This is Whiting Bay, site of the longest pier on the Clyde."

And after a short pause: "But it's no' there any longer."

READER Jock Clark in Kilmacolm has just returned from a touring holiday to Italy, Slovenia and Croatia. An elderly lady on the trip was often seen carrying a large box around with her.

Jock's curiosity eventually got the better of him and he asked what it contained.

"It's a cyclamen plant," she explained. "I didn't trust anyone at home to look after it while I was away."

A STIRLING reader on holiday in a Texas diner heard a local, about to tuck into a monster steak, declare: "Vegetarian – an old Indian word for lousy hunter."

DEREK McCANN in Aberdeen was flying from Atlanta to Orlando in the United States when a family of four behind him in the queue were told there were only two remaining seats. At that the grumpy

mother announced she and her daughter would take them, and her husband and son could get a later flight, for all she cared.

Later on board the plane Derek heard the woman ask a steward if he knew what had happened to her missing husband and son.

Says Derek: "When the attendant told her they were in fact up in business class, her face was a picture."

READER Phyllis Cleghorn in Stirling was going on holiday to Jersey and phoned her bank to let them know so that her credit card would work there, and not be blocked for unusual activity.

After explaining to the call centre worker on some foreign shore that she was going to the Channel Islands for a week, she was put on hold until a supervisor came on the line and asked: "Where did you say you were going for a week?"

When Phyllis repeated that she was going to the Channel Islands there was a pause before the supervisor replied: "Oh. My colleague said you were going to China and Ireland."

A READER visiting Lord Nelson's *HMS Victory* in Portsmouth tells us that the tour guides naturally take the history of the ship very seriously. And our reader tells us it just had to be a Scottish voice that shouted out on the tour, when the guide reverently pointed out the plaque on the spot where Nelson fell: "I'm no surprised. I nearly tripped ower it ma'sell."

NOT MANY Scots are great linguists it has to be said. But a reader in a branch of Superdrug in Glasgow's city centre had remembered enough French to realise that the French girl in front of him was saying to her pal: "Why do they need suntan lotion here?"

HOLIDAY problems we had never thought about. Neil Gibson and wife flew off on holiday, and his good lady, not wishing to leave the car keys lying around an empty house, planked them in the oven. The only problem was, she hadn't counted on dutiful daughter coming round to the house the day before they returned to bake a birthday cake – which came out to the aroma of melted plastic, and a car outside that could no longer be opened.

CHRISTINE PACIONE, of Milton of Campsie, overheard a blonde, tattooed lady at a holiday spot asking about going on the sunset cruise. When asked when she would like to go, she replied: "Sunday morning."

18.
It's The Law

IN GLASGOW'S Barlinnie Jail, the most prized possession is an illicit mobile phone. There is even a chair with a built-in X-ray machine to check felons for a hidden model. Dead pigeons, with mobile phones concealed in the carrion, are even thrown over the walls for the incarcerated to retrieve.

So we wonder how much the prison officer was joking when, before the start of David Haymen performing Rony Bridge's autobiographical one-man play *Six and a Tanner* inside Barlinnie, he asked the inmates attending to switch off their mobile phones during the performance.

A GLASGOW lawyer phones to tell us a colleague was in court trying to butter up a witness by telling him: "You're a very bright, smart witness."

And the chap replied: "Thank you. If I wasn't under oath I'd repay the compliment."

A BBC film about Scotland's famous safecracker Gentle Johnny Ramensky, reminds retired reporter Gordon Airs of interviewing another safeblower, Paddy Meehan, who told him that he did a bank job with Johnny towards the end of his criminal career.

Searching about in the dark for the safe, Johnny whispered that he had found it. Recalled Paddy: "I padded up and saw it was a fridge. I opened the door and the light came on. He said his eyes weren't what they used to be, and I said, 'You're no' kidding.'

"When we found the safe I let him put on the plastic explosive. He was always so finicky – he just wanted the door to swing open perfectly. I packed in a lot more and he complained that it would blow the door off. I said: 'Listen, it's no oor safe.'"

OH YES, the London riots. A London hoodie contacts us: "I'm told a police van rushing to the riots hit two looters. One was thrown through the windscreen and the other was knocked over a wall.

"The Met charged the first one with breaking and entering, and the second with leaving the scene of an accident."

YOU HAVE to be wary of what appears to be a bargain offered on the Internet. Said one chap in a Glasgow pub: "I paid £200 to a firm which guaranteed to make me rich.

"Turned out they changed my name to Richard by deed poll."

RETIRED police inspector turned crime writer Les Brown tells us that many years ago in the Gorbals, new police recruits were taken on the beat and led into the cellar of the vast Co-op headquarters in Morrison Street where the coffins were stored.

Says Les: "After a few minutes the lid of a coffin would slide sideways and a shrouded figure, which was of course another cop, sat up.

"The practice came to a sudden end when a young cop struck the shrouded figure with his baton before exiting the building."

OUR LUNCH stories remind a lawyer: "Advocate Donald Findlay tells of a junior counsel assisting him in a trial at the High Court in Glasgow whom he sent to fetch something for lunch. 'Nip up to M&S. Get a tuna and sweetcorn sandwich for me and something for yourself.' The youth returned and gave Donald his lunch and 50p change. Donald pointed out he had give him a £20 note and had expected rather more.

"'But you told me to get something for myself,' replied the lad.

"'Well what did you get – caviar, foie gras?'

"'No, a shirt.'"

WE MENTIONED Rony Bridges' play *Six and a Tanner* being performed at Barlinnie Prison. It subsequently was put on at Greenock Prison.

A chuffed Rony told writer and actor Tony Roper afterwards: "One lifer told me it was the most powerful piece of drama he had ever seen."

"To be fair," replied Tony cautiously, "he probably doesn't get out much."

OUR LONDON contact phones to tell us the excuse used by one of the rioters appearing in court. Apparently the miscreant blamed his mobile phone's predictive text and claimed all he had tried to do was text his pals to ask if they wanted to meet up that night for a pint.

One chap, with a 42-inch plasma telly balanced on the front of his pushbike, claimed it was his satnav.

And another was dubbed the city's worst looter. Apparently he ran into Argos and escaped with a dozen catalogues.

YES THE London riots were shocking, so we don't believe our London contact who told us his neighbour announced: "I feel bad about turning my kids into the police for being involved in the looting.

"You see they were innocent, but having them locked up is a lot cheaper than paying for a child minder during the school holidays."

AND TRYING to find something positive in it all is Eric Scot out in Bondi who opines: "Now that the Metropolitan police are getting the hang of it, they might be ready for a resumption of the home internationals."

THE ENGLISH riots were being discussed at an Ayrshire golf club this week, where one club member opined: "Did you hear the rioters in court arguing that 'everyone else was doing it' and 'I needed more money'.

"Well we've heard all these excuses before – from MPs."

AND FINALLY on the riots, a London court contact tells us: "One of the looters was fined for taking goods from a DFS furniture store. But he doesn't have to pay anything until 2013."

FUTURE productions at the Royal Conservatoire of Scotland – the old RSAMD in Glasgow – were being discussed at a staff planning meeting when the staging of *Tommy the Musical* next March came up. A bemused member of staff asked if Tommy would be out of prison in time for the opening night and whether he had given his approval for the show.

It was then gently explained to her that they were talking about the Pete Townshend rock musical based on The Who's 1969 double album, as opposed to the life story of Pollok naughty-boy turned politician Tommy Sheridan.

THE HERALD reported that Celtic chairman John Reid had complained to First Minister Alex Salmond about John Wilson, the Hearts fan who was cleared of assaulting Celtic manager Neil Lennon.

Reader Joe Hughes in Johnstone explains what actually happened in court that day.

"Just before the jury foreman delivered the verdict, the defence lawyer asked him: 'Who is the best Celtic winger ever – Jimmy Johnstone or Davie Provan?'

"'Not Provan,' replied the foreman."

19.
The Fairer Sex

It goes without saying that women can have the sharpest and funniest tongues around.

AN AYRSHIRE reader out with friends heard a cacophony of shouting and spied a hen party touring the pubs.

The bride-to-be was not young, but the slogan emblazoned across her party gear read: "Half a hunner. But still a stunner!"

A WEST END woman returning from a company party with her husband asked him: "Have I ever told you how handsome and sexy and totally irresistible to all women you are?"

"Why, no," replied her deeply flattered husband.

"Then what," she added, "gave you that stupid idea at the party?"

FAVOURITE Twitter message we've read this week: "My husband complains I put too much information on Twitter. Clearly, his haemorrhoids are making him cranky."

THE WOMAN having coffee with friends in a grey, drizzly Glasgow was perhaps being a bit harsh when she confided: "When I told Derek I didn't want to see him any more, he told me I would never meet someone like him again.

"I told him that's what I was hoping for."

A READER back from holiday in Guernsey relates that some fun-loving, young Glasgow women were staying at the same hotel. One morning, they were discussing what they got up to the night before. One of them was being accused of getting over-amorous with a chap, but she defended herself: "Leave us alone. Nothing happened – we were just talking, that's all."

"Don't talk tripe, Mags," retorted a pal. "You had his shirt aff faster than a nurse applying CPR."

A GROUP of young women were overheard discussing how lazy their boyfriends were over a bottle of Pinot Grigio in Glasgow's West End.

The winner was the girl who alleged: "My Jackie's so lazy, even his smoke alarm has a snooze button on it."

"NO, I DON'T get jealous seeing my ex-boyfriend with someone else," said the woman in the West End bar to her friends who had spotted the ex coming in the door.

"My mother always taught me to give my old toys to those less fortunate."

A READER overhears two women in Glasgow discussing a mutual friend's new boyfriend, with one explaining that the chap is rather on the large side.

"How big is he?" asked her friend.

"Put it this way," she replied. "He needs a boomerang to put a belt on."

"DO YOU ever miss the ex?" a woman meeting her girlfriends for a drink asked in Glasgow's West End.

"Oh all the time," replied one of her pals. "You wouldn't believe how much."

"But I thought you hated his guts?" replied the first woman.

"Wait a minute," replied her pal. "Did you say 'ex' or 'sex'?"

A WOMAN having coffee with friends in Glasgow was discussing her new boyfriend and mentioned she had reservations about him having such a hairy back. "How hairy is it?" eagerly asked a pal.

"Put it this way," she replied, "I'm worried that if we go on holiday this summer, animal rights activists will throw red paint over him."

WOMEN drivers – won't hear a word against them. However, John Bannerman tells us that when his wife was learning to drive in Kilmarnock she had to react when the car in front of her at traffic lights began to reverse towards her. But instead of sounding the horn, she chapped on her windscreen to attract the driver's attention.

TWO WOMEN catching up in a West End bar were watching the married chap at the bar fiddle absentmindedly with his wedding ring. "What do you think he's doing?" remarked one. "Trying to work out the combination?"

FOLK trying to talk posh reminds Mary McNeill in Lanarkshire of an aspirational friend who, when travelling by bus to the village of Stane near Shotts, would ask for "one to Stone" which always led to her being asked to repeat it.

A READER overhears a Glasgow woman tell her pals over a coffee: "In the evening I can hear any leftover cake, and sometimes ice cream, calling to me from the fridge.

"Broccoli is strangely silent."

"MY DAUGHTER," said the woman having coffee with friends in Edinburgh this week, "has just texted saying 'call me ASAP'.

"I think," she told her friends, "I'll just stick to Jennifer."

ANDREW GILMOUR tells us he was on a bus in Maryhill when the wee wummin behind him asked her pal if she liked oysters, but she replied that she had never tried them.

"Ah think they're great," persisted the first woman. "Oor James brings us in bags o' them an we stick them in the freezer."

"How dae ye eat them?"

"Open them an fill them wi' ice cream."

"Does that no make the ice cream taste o' fish?"

"Naw it's no they oysters. It's the wans ye get in the ice cream shoap."

A BEARSDEN reader admires the fortitude of wee Glasgow wummin. When she came out of the Tesco store on Maryhill Road last week she passed one such local lady who was bent double while trying to make headway against the gale-force wind. Their eyes met and the wee wummin, almost going one step backwards for every step forwards, remarked: "Aye it's a good dryin' day."

OUR STORIES of age mistakes reminds a female reader of being out walking in bad weather with her hood up when a passing police car stopped, and the young officer asked her her name and where she lived.

She tells us: "After my bemused responses he explained that I fitted the description of a woman reported missing from the local nursing home.

"I threw down my hood and told him I was only in my early fifties. He quickly jumped back into his car with a look of fear in his eyes that he may be assaulted by an even more irate and humiliated middle-aged, drookit woman."

AGED aunts continued. George Morton in Newton Mearns recalls: "My aunt was visiting from Wales. She described her journey in her son's BMW as very smooth, and that her son hadn't exceeded 30mph all the way up. Later her son confided she had been looking at the rev counter and not the speedometer. At 3000 revs a Beamer is travelling at 90mph."

CONGRATULATIONS to Glasgow City FC for winning the Scottish Women's Premier League for the fourth year in a row. The women's game has come on leaps and bounds since an old buffer once told us:

"Women's football will never catch on. How will you ever get eleven women to go outside in the same outfit?"

THREE loud office-workers having a drink after work on Friday in Glasgow were en route to their staff Christmas party when one was asked if she would kiss her boss under the mistletoe.

"I wouldn't even kiss him under anaesthetic," she replied.

ANDREW STALKER tells us about police in Falkirk using a sniffer dog at club queues to detect drugs. When the dog stopped next to a group of females and barked, one of the girls broke down, confessing she was under eighteen, but how could the dog possibly know?

It turned out it had detected drugs on a chap behind her and was not, as she had thought, trained to work out folk's ages.

WITH Christmas approaching, an Airdrie reader tells us about taking his aged mum out to a local hotel for Christmas lunch last year, where she surprised him by asking: "Why would anyone bring their budgie with them?"

As thoughts of old ladies sitting there with cages on the table filled his mind, he asked what she was on about.

She pointed at a sign at the door which read: "No prams or buggies."

20.
At The Church

Weddings, funerals, church services . . . even there, a smile or two can be discovered.

CHRIS THORNHILL in Ardfern tells us about the Highland funeral in winter when the two gravediggers were standing to one side, stamping their feet and patting their arms to try to keep warm, while waiting for the end of the graveside service.

As the mourners turned to leave, one of them approached the cold gravediggers and asked: "Do you chaps take a dram?" When they eagerly answered in the affirmative, the mourner pointed back at the grave and told them: "Well let that be a dreadful warning to you."

OUR SCOTTISH funeral stories remind a reader of attending one such service where the poignancy of the occasion was enhanced by a lone piper playing a lament outside the church as the mourners went in.

The moment was perhaps spoiled, she tells us, by a colleague of the deceased, who had flown up from London, who muttered as he saw the piper: "Damn buskers. Don't they know there's a time and a place?"

WE ASKED for your funeral stories, and Annie McQuiston recalls: "We were attending an elderly great aunt's funeral and the CD was playing 'The White Cliffs of Dover'. All very solemn as the curtains closed at the crematorium until the next song came belting out, which was 'Wish Me Luck as You Wave Me Goodbye'.

"May just request this for my own."

AND FRANCES WOODWARD in Mirfield, Yorkshire, recalls: "My friend worked for an undertakers and was told a wee wummin would come in for a last look at her husband before committal the next day, and would she be alright taking her down to the viewing room?

"Duly complying with this, she was startled when the woman asked for the teeth back he had in his mouth, as they shared them and she wanted to wear them at the funeral."

RUSSELL SMITH tells us: "I was told by a minister friend that as the curtains closed and the coffin began to disappear during a service in the crematorium, a voice wafted up, 'That's me away then.'

"This turned out to be an employee who had asked to leave early to play a snooker match and had been told he could leave as soon as that part of the proceedings ended."

ALISTAIR FULTON tells us of the butcher who asked for the Johann Sebastian Bach cantata "Schafe können sicher weiden" to be played at his funeral. It is known in English of course as "Sheep May Safely Graze".

And Catol Bannon tells us: "I attended a cremation where the family had chosen 'Don't Forsake Me Oh My Darling' from the film *High Noon* as this was a particular favourite of the deceased.

"However, at the crucial moment, just as the coffin was going slowly past, the attendant had selected the wrong track on the CD and out boomed, 'Rollin', rollin', rollin', keep them dawgies rollin'. . .'"

VALERIE LANG tells us about attending a service at a Lanarkshire crematorium, where the snow and ice made the car park treacherous. Says Valerie: "Exchanging pleasantries with a lady in the hushed waiting room, I raised the subject of the weather conditions, to which she replied, 'I know. You'd think they'd put ashes down or something.'

"The look of horror that crossed her face was followed by stifled giggles by all those around."

OUR MENTION of eulogies reminds Gus Furrie in East Kilbride of being at a funeral where the minister described the deceased as being a chief petty officer in the navy when he was younger.

Gus heard a voice in the pew behind him muttering: "Goodness, he's been promoted since he died."

OUR TALE of the church service reminds Gerry Burke in Dumbarton of the yarn: "Wee fella, returning home in back seat of the car in surly, uncommunicative mood after baby sister's baptism in local church, resists repeated attempts by dad to source the problem. Finally, in high dudgeon, the lad explains, 'The priest said he was glad we were going to be brought up in a nice, Christian home. But I want to stay with you.'"

WE ARE always impressed by the lengths the clergy will go to at funerals in order to be as positive as they can about the departed. An Ayrshire reader tells us she witnessed her parish priest trying to get round the infrequent visits to church by the deceased, by declaring in his eulogy: "Mary never completely lost her faith – she never missed an edition of *Songs of Praise*."

A READER says when he was at Sunday School he thought the teacher had said that Jesus had been put to his death, not by Pontius Pilate, but an "unconscious pilot".

"Until I was twelve," he tells us, "I thought Jesus had died in a helicopter accident."

WHEN the Christian period of Lent started we were reminded of the chap in the Glasgow pub being asked by mates what he was giving up for Lent.

"My New Year's resolutions," he replied.

THE MINISTER at Motherwell South Church was introducing the story of Samson and Delilah to the children in the congregation and, trying to involve them as much as possible, she asked: "What do you know about Samson?" Alas the story of the hair cut didn't immediately come to mind with one young lad who, trying to remember where he thought he had seen the name before, put up his hand and shouted: "He made oor telly miss."

WE ASKED for your Scottish wedding stories, and Rev. James MacEwan at Abernethy Parish Church tells us: "Some years ago I was conducting a wedding in the church in Advie, near Grantown-on-Spey.

"A small child was competing with me for the ears of the congregation and took his mother's full attention.

"Just as I asked if anyone knew any reason why the couple could not lawfully be joined in marriage, the mother rose to exit with her child.

"Every head turned in alarm."

JIM GRIER in Saltcoats tells us about a recent wedding in Ayrshire where the nervous bride, struggling to keep a steady hand while signing the register, was advised by the minister that it might help if she put her weight on it. After the ceremony, the minister noticed that after her signature she had added "8st 7lb".

SCOTTISH rhyming slang that doesn't travel. Rosy Gillies on Arran tells us her gran was working in an Ayrshire hotel where an English couple were staying before going to a local wedding. When she asked where the wedding was, the English chap replied: "Some place called the Pineapple – sounds quite posh."

Rosy's gran felt duty bound to explain to them that it was actually the local chapel where the ceremony was taking place.

THE POPE arrived in Glasgow, and reader Jennifer Wilkie reminisces about her father-in-law building a wooden altar for the previous Pope when he visited a hospital near Edinburgh. After dismantling it, he cut it into 10in pieces, varnished them, branded "Pope John Paul stood here" on them and gave them to charities to auction. Unfortunately, says Jennifer, demand was so high that he had to sneak off to B&Q to buy more wood, and his grandson has now worked out that the wooden altar must have covered about fourteen square miles to accommodate all the pieces.

ALL THIS talk of Glasgow and religion reminds a reader of the classic – that is, old – yarn of the charismatic preacher visiting Glasgow. He asked a young man in the congregation what was bothering him. "My hearing," the chap replied.

So the preacher laid his hands over the young fellow's ears, asked the congregation to pray with him to God, took his hands away and asked the man: "How is your hearing now?"

"I don't know," the chap replied. "I'm not due at the sheriff court until tomorrow."

IAN DEUCHAR in Milngavie tells us: "A group of seniors fore-gathered at my local golf club when someone asked if we were looking forward to watching the Royal Wedding.

"I said I had a garden wall to paint, and another old boy asked if he could come and watch my paint drying."

A GLASGOW reader watching the American news channel CNN on his telly got annoyed when they referred to Prince William and his girlfriend Kate meeting in "St Andrews, England".

He thought about complaining, he says, until every student they interviewed there was an "uppperclass English oik giving it yahoo" so decided not to bother.

"DID YOU see the interview with Sarah Ferguson, Prince Andrew's ex," said the chap in the pub, "where she said that missing the Royal Wedding was difficult?"

"I know what she means," replied his pal. "It seemed to be on every sodding channel."

A YOUNG lady phones to tell us how to work out if you are posher than new royal bride Kate Middleton.

The formula apparently is to multiply your weekly glasses of wine by the number of Apple products you own, then subtract your total number of tattoos multiplied by the number of missing teeth.

WITH that wedding in London, Americans were showing their interest in the royal family.

Glasgow-born talk show host in America Craig Ferguson told his audience: "Queen Elizabeth has turned eighty-five. There was an awkward moment when she closed her eyes to make a wish and Prince Charles asked, 'Is she dead?'"

THE ROYAL Wedding gags are now in abundance. "I've just bought a lovely Prince Charles commemorative teapot," phones one reader.

"It never reigns, but it pours."

READERS enjoyed the news story about Prince William visiting the Faslane submarine base on the Clyde and the chief petty officer who, when asked by the prince what it was like serving on submarines, replied: "There are ups and downs."

21.
Sport

There could never be a book about Scottish humour that missed out sport.

A MEMBER of staff at John Smith's university bookshop in Glasgow took an order from a Chinese student named Wan Fan.

He thought that the fact he lived in the student village next to Partick Thistle's ground at Firhill was particularly apposite.

FORMER Aberdeen footballer Duncan Shearer tells in his autobiography, *Shearer Wonderland*, of six players on a pre-season trip to Austria being fined for staying out boozing until four in the morning.

Duncan was feeling smug when he phoned his wife as he was not one of the six.

Instead, the first thing she asked was how come he and pal Billy Dodds were not involved as it was not like them to miss a good night out, so what had they been up to?

IAN BARNETT tells us: "Former referee Willie Young was guest speaker at a golf day at Old Prestwick when he told of a man two up with three to play in the club championship.

"His phone rang and the police told him his wife had been found hanging on the washing line in his garden.

"After some thought he told them: 'Thanks for that. If it rains can you bring her in?'"

OUR MENTION of football ground humour reminds Keddie Law in Montrose of when Dundee played Celtic in the SPL on the last game of the season in which they had already been relegated. Celtic fans sang the Vera Lynn classic: "We'll meet again, don't know where, don't know when."

BARRIE CRAWFORD tells us: "When I took the referees' course, we were told of a linesman officiating at Fir Park who raised his flag to indicate that a Motherwell player was offside.

"From the terracing behind him came the exhortation, 'Haw, linesman, stick the flag up yer ****!'

"The said linesman turned round and addressed his abuser with, 'Ah canny . . . it's full of whistles.'"

A MEMBER of the Tartan Army was heard complaining: "When I'm getting amorous with the wife, I used to tell her to lie back and think of Scotland.

"But that just gets us both really depressed these days."

MANCHESTER UNITED boss Sir Alex Ferguson, giving a lecture on leadership at the esteemed Royal College of Physicians and Surgeons of Glasgow, told his audience of a quiz between coaching staff and players on a foreign trip.

The coaches were leading with one question to go, when the players were asked which artist painted *Sunflowers*.

Given the blank looks from the players, the coaches were confident of victory, only for former player Nicky Butt to shout out: "Van Gogh!"

Sir Alex, who does not take kindly to losing, barked: "How the hell did you know that?"

Nicky merely replied: "I have two in my house."

SPORTS journalist Robert Philip, in his book *Scottish Sporting Legends*, tells the tale of legendary Liverpool manager Bill Shankley berating forward Tony Hateley for his lack of talent. Defending himself, Tony replied: "You have to admit I'm great in the air."

But Shankley barked back: "I'll grant you that son, but so was Douglas Bader and he had two better legs than you'll ever have."

INCIDENTALLY, when writing about the great games of golf that have been played at St Andrews, Robert recalls the barman at the Jigger Inn overlooking the Old Course who, according to legend, spent the 1960s selling off the pub's entire collection of stools and tables at the rate of one a week to visiting Americans, all nicely engraved: "Tom Morris Drank Here. 26 June 1859."

OUR STORY of former Liverpool manager Bill Shankley decrying a player's ability reminds Derek McCann in Aberdeen: "The story goes that when Martin O'Neill was Celtic manager he told an underperforming Rafael Scheidt, 'You know, you remind me of me as a player – and I'm forty-five.'"

DREADFUL result for Scotland at Hampden against the Czech Republic. Murray Robertson had taken his partner's nine-year-old son, whose father is Norwegian, to the game. As they walked away from the park, an auld fella ruffled the youngster's hair and told him not to worry about it.

"It's OK," replied the young Norwegian. "I was told that if I'm going to support Scotland I'll have to be prepared for disappointment."

THE DIVING Czech player Jan Rezek, who conned the referee for the crucial last-minute penalty, was much discussed on the Tartan Army online messageboard.

Fan Jamesie Cottar – not his real name we suspect – commented: "To blame Rezek for diving is like blaming a puppy for taking a dump on the carpet. It's what professional footballers do (I mean dive and cheat, not take a dump on the carpet)."

BLAME Diary correspondent John Dyer for this one.

"What is llddddlddwlddllllldldldl?" he asks. "Is it a) a market town in South Wales, b) a chorus from a Rolf Harris song, or c) the results of Rangers' last twenty-two games in Europe?"

THE NEWSPAPERS were full of the story of Brazilian starlet Neymar claiming he was racially abused and had a banana thrown at him at the friendly match against Scotland.

But as Tartan Army footsoldier John Daly tells us: "Neymar should have done a bit more research before accusing Scotland fans of racism. A Scotsman with fruit? Aye, right."

MATT VALLANCE, visiting the new St Mirren park, noticed that the nearby Buddies Snack Bar offered a full breakfast for £3, but you could get a larger "Mark Yardley Breakfast" for £3.70 with almost double the contents.

Mark of course was a St Mirren legend in the late eighties who scored over seventy goals for the club, but was, it has to be said, a bit on the bulky side towards the end of his career.

Says Matt: "Only in Scotland is fame so fleeting. All those goals for St Mirren and how is big Yards remembered? As a fatty."

MONEY is tight in Scottish football with attendances dropping, corporate hospitality falling away and television money being cut. A Lanarkshire reader tells us he was talking to his pal, a professional footballer, who told him: "I asked my agent if he could get me a new contract.

"He said in the current climate the only contract he could get me would be £30 a month with 200 minutes free airtime and 500 free texts."

RACEHORSES in Britain have to be registered with names only up to eighteen characters long, and any names that are considered rude or insulting are rejected.

Some cheeky owners try to get round the ban however, and horse-racing website lovetheraces.com tells us that among the attempted names which were thrown out by the authorities were Hugh Gass Kisser, Ima Goodlay and Anna Reksik.

Racing officials can't spot everything, though, and among the names which have been accepted are the old school-boy one Hoof Hearted, the rather clever Peony's Envy, and the one many racegoers look for but never find, Geespot.

"BEER company Carling," our English football contact tells us, "must be gutted that after sponsoring the Carling Cup, Birmingham's best player in the final was their goalkeeper Foster."

And he added: "Some Arsenal fans were seen taking flares into Wembley. Apparently they were the ones they were wearing the last time they won anything."

A JOKE for football fans only. Rangers former manager Walter Smith, who was accused of being overly defensively-minded when in charge, needed his roof repaired. After a builder went up to have a look at the damage, he climbed down and told Walter it would cost £4,000 to repair, which the Rangers manager agreed was fair. However, as the builder had to buy tiles, he told Walter: "I'll need two up front and the other two when the job's done."

"Two up front?" screamed Walter. "Are you off your head?"

AS ENGLAND licks its wounds over the World Cup knock-back, a fan in London phones to tell us: "After England were stitched up by FIFA in the World Cup bid, we should follow Scotland's example and just refuse to even try to qualify in future."

SOMEONE got a book for Christmas we reckon. Dave Martin was at the Old Firm New Year derby game when he heard an exasperated Rangers fan claim the team had lost the plot.

A fellow fan piped up: "Lafferty's no just lost the plot – he couldnae spot one in a Dan Brown novel."

NATURALLY we had to investigate the big Ayrshire Junior football game at the weekend, Cumnock v Auchinleck Talbot, which shamefully involved mounted police officers clearing fighting fans off the pitch.

However, one old-timer, a veteran of over fifty years of such clashes, told us: "Only one red card and only one arrest – this was a quiet Cumnock v Talbot match."

IT SEEMS the worldwide web is even changing traditional football chants. Partick Thistle fan Foster Evans couldn't wait to tell Facebook friends around the world that Thistle had won 6-1 at the weekend.

But as a fellow football fan replied: "Post when you're winning! You only post when you're winning . . ."

GORDON PEDEN was with the Tartan Army in Dublin for the Scotland game, and strolling around town afterwards, basking in the glory of the win, he had to shout a warning to a friend from Edinburgh who had inadvertently strolled in front of a vehicle on Dublin's Luas, the city's light railway system.

Gordon was just wondering afterwards, if he hadn't shouted the warning, would anyone ever believe the heading: "Edinburgh man struck by tram"?

RANGERS legend Willie Johnston, in Glasgow for the team's Europa League tie against Sporting Lisbon, recalls being at Caesar's Palace in Las Vegas with England player Alan Ball where they got annoyed by loud pages being broadcast from reception.

Ball went across and asked reception to page: "1966 World Cup winner Alan Ball to meet him at reception". As Ball strolled back over to Willie, reception was engulfed with English visitors hoping to meet a World Cup hero, and Ball told Willie: "That'll keep them occupied."

AS CELTIC fans endlessly debate refereeing decisions, Ian Duff in Inverness tells us about a disputed goal at Partick Thistle's ground. The referee appeared to appease the opposition by going over to consult his linesman. However, fans in the front row of the stand could hear the ref say to the official: "Fine day, isn't it?"

The linesman said, "It is that," while nodding his head vigorously in agreement.

The ref blows for a goal and heads for the centre spot to restart the game.

MORE football nostalgia, as reader Russell Pettigrew, after the fuss over the Rangers penalty against Celtic, reminds us of the imperious

Tom "Tiny" Wharton refereeing an Old Firm game when he turned down a loud Celtic claim for a penalty.

Says Russell: "Bobby Lennox pursued him, complaining bitterly that it was definitely a penalty, to which Tiny replied, 'I think, Mr Lennox, that when you read tomorrow's papers you'll find that it wasn't.'"